THE JOY OF
BEADING

THE JOY OF
BEADING

Anna Borrelli

MORE THAN 50 EASY PROJECTS
FOR JEWELRY • FLOWERS •
DECOR • ACCESSORIES

Translated by Rosanna M. Giammanco Frongia, Ph.D.

Watson-Guptill Publications / New York

Created by Studio Sperandeo - Milan
Series editor: Cristina Sperandeo
Graphic Design: Mimola
Photographs: Massimo Bottura with the assistance of Giulia Mondelli
Translation: Rosanna M. Giammanco Frongia, Ph.D.
Typesetting: Michael Shaw

First published in the United States in 2005 by
Watson-Guptill Publications,
a division of VNU Business Media, Inc.,
770 Broadway, New York, NY 10003

Library of Congress Cataloging-in-Publication Data
Borrelli, Anna.
  The joy of beading : more than 50 easy projects for jewelry, flowers,
décor, accessories / Anna Borrelli ; translated by Rosanna M.
Giammanco Frongia.
    p. cm.
  Includes bibliographical references and index.
  ISBN 0-8230-2648-5 (alk. paper)
  1. Beadwork. I. Title.
  TT860.B68 2005
  745.58'2--dc22

                                        2005011836

Printed and bound
by Artes Gráficas Toledo, S.A.U.,
Spain

Metric Conversions
Limited space makes it impossible to give both standard and metric
measurements. While amounts of beads and bead sizes are given in
millimeters and centimeters, as is customary, lengths of wire, twine,
and thread are expressed in standard measurements.

To convert inches to centimeters, multiply the number by 2.5.
To convert feet to meters, multiply the number by 0.3.

To Linda and Ignazio,
my wonderful parents

I am grateful to the Mayer
Company of Milan for supplying
all the materials I used in mak-
ing the projects for this book.

First printing, 2005

4 5 6 7 8 9 / 10 09 08 07

Introduction

The love of personal adornment and home decoration has always been part of human history. This book wants to communicate this creative impulse to the reader. It is a practical manual that guides the reader to experiment in creating jewelry, ornamental objects, and accessories using beads, those small slivers of light that exert such a powerful attraction on all of us. Because they are versatile and easy to use, beads are the perfect material to help us translate all the nuances of our personality, even the most hidden, into the creation of unique objects. My enthusiasm for this craft dates from adolescence and has continued to grow in the ten years and more of my professional involvement in beadwork, a craft that is a constant source of gratification and growth.

Table of Contents

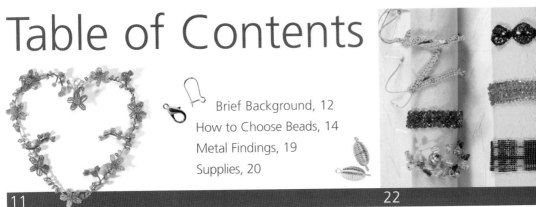

Brief Background, 12
How to Choose Beads, 14
Metal Findings, 19
Supplies, 20

11

A Word of Advice

22

Jewelry

34

Cloud Necklace

36

Lariat Necklace

38

Organza Necklace

40

Bead and Cord Necklace

54

String Tie

56

Blooming Necklace

58

Crocheted Earrings

60

Crocheted Bracelet

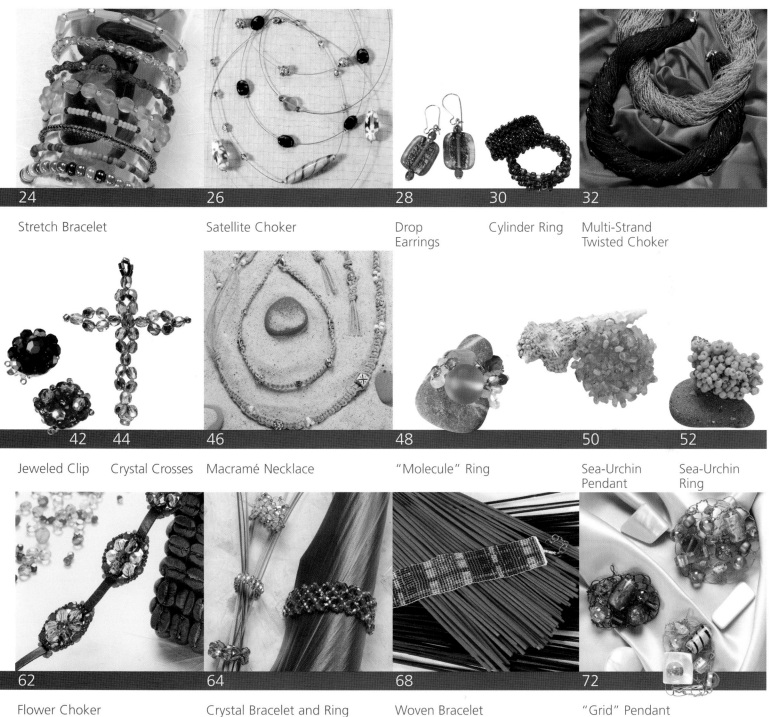

24 Stretch Bracelet

26 Satellite Choker

28 Drop Earrings

30 Cylinder Ring

32 Multi-Strand Twisted Choker

42 Jeweled Clip

44 Crystal Crosses

46 Macramé Necklace

48 "Molecule" Ring

50 Sea-Urchin Pendant

52 Sea-Urchin Ring

62 Flower Choker

64 Crystal Bracelet and Ring

68 Woven Bracelet

72 "Grid" Pendant

74 "Grid" Ring

76 Tassels

80 **Flowers**

90 Wisteria

92 Poppy

94 Zinnia

96 Olive Tree

106 Lavender

108 Grape Vine

110 **Accessories**

82 Stalk of Wheat

84 Tiny Roses

86 Daisy

88 Iris

98 Peach Tree

100 Red Rose

102 Carnation

104 Water Lily

112 Beaded Picture Frame

114 Lamp Shade

116 Flower Picture Frame

118 Purse Handles

Contents

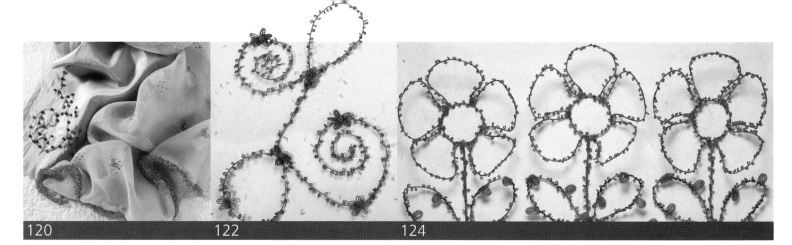

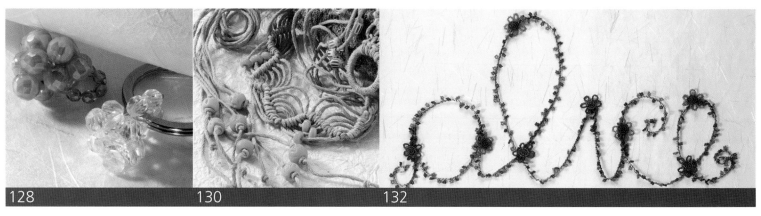

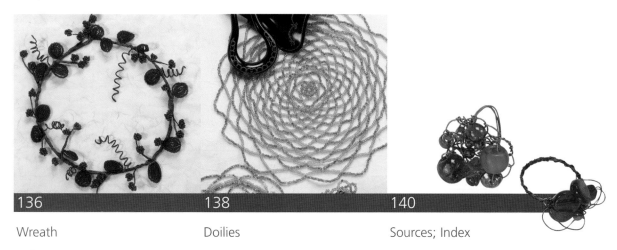

120 Beaded Scarf

122 Alphabet Letters

124 Flower Clothes Hooks

128 Key Ring

130 Beaded Cord Belt

132 Write a Name

136 Wreath

138 Doilies

140 Sources; Index

A Word of Advice

Time Required for Each Project

Before you begin, you should keep in mind that the time indicated for each project varies depending on your skill and the care you bring to the project. Still, as you will soon discover as you read on, many of the more unusual projects actually take little time to make.

Flexibility in Using the Materials

Given the wide assortment of beads on the market, you might find yourself using beads of a slightly different size than what is suggested here. Therefore, please remember that the best way to proceed is to adapt the findings and materials to the size of the beads you are using. For example, if your project calls for beads all of the same diameter and size, all you need to do is choose a wire of the appropriate thickness. But if the project you are working on calls for beads of different sizes or shapes, you may need to change the number of beads required, because diameter and facets affect the lines of the design. No need to worry, though: you will find that as you look at the illustrations in this manual, you will naturally adapt your work as required. Simply follow the harmony in the design and the instructions, and do not worry if at first you are not totally successful: we learn also by our mistakes.

Brief Background

Beads were the earliest decorations worn by men and women, and their use and creation has been traced back thousands of years. The oldest beads were found in prehistoric tombs and date back to the Neanderthal age, about 38,000 BC. By then, our distant ancestors had learned how to work animal bones and teeth into the pendants that were found in prehistoric tombs, proof of the importance they held for primitive man. It was believed, in fact, that ornaments made with parts of killed animals transmitted the animal's strength to the wearer. In the succeeding millennia, beads became essential decorative elements of practically all peoples and all cultures of the world. In Italy, Venice is undoubtedly the cradle of glass beads: manufacturing began there in the ninth century or thereabouts and became a flourishing industry in the thirteenth century. As a matter of fact, the city rulers confined the manufacture of beads and glasswork to the Island of Murano to protect Venice from the risk of fires from kilns that worked around the clock. Another reason for relegating it to an island was the desire to keep the production process secret.

At various times in history, beads also served as exchange currency. On this subject, one of the oldest testimonies is from Christopher Columbus: when he discovered the New World, he offered to the native tribes strings of beads as a token of his good intentions, thus winning over their friendship. Lamentably, beads were also used in exploitative situations, such as the slave trade: according to detailed price lists that have survived, many of the fifteen million African slaves who were sent to the Americas between 1500 and 1867 were bought by slave traders with European glass beads.

In one way or another, the story of every civilization is linked to beads. For example, the American Indians, who had no written language, used beaded belts, called wampum, on which they wove the narratives of important events. The people of Tibet wore turquoise beads as protection from evil spirits. Today, in the West in particular, beads are no longer linked to any specific symbolism but change and adapt in accordance with current fashions.

How to Choose Beads

Once you begin your first beadwork project, you will realize that there is an almost endless array of beads to choose from. To help you in your selection, we present in the following pages an overview of the types of beads currently on the market, their colors, and brief descriptions.

Seed beads. Known as *conterie* in Italy, these are the tiny, "classic" beads. They were originally made from glass canes that were hollowed and pulled by hand by the kiln master, then finished by Venetian women who were known as *impirarasse* from the Venetian *impirar*, to string. They come in several shapes: *round; bugle* (thin, round tubular beads of varying length but longer than 3mm); *2-cut* or *3-cut* beads—they are thin, short (2 or 3mm) tubes that may be faceted; *hex-cuts* (6-sided beads); *triangle* beads (Japanese beads with triangular cross-sections); etc. Manufacturing today still follows the "pulled glass" technique, producing thousands of identical objects in a very short time. In addition to seed beads, the following, larger types of beads are also on the market.

Crystals. Crystal-cut glass is produced in several countries, but the best known and most expensive is undoubtedly Swarovski crystal, so named for its founder, Daniel Swarovski. A young crystal cutter who worked in his father's shop, Swarovski soon realized the importance of speeding up the process of production. In 1892, he patented a machine that precision-cut crystal. By steam-applying a wafer-thin layer of metal, he then experimented with new coloring effects on the cut and polished crystal, creating the so-called aurora borealis effect. The crystals normally used to make beads are not pure, which is why, technically, they are called "half-crystals."

Lampwork beads. Originally, Venetian craftsmen made this type of bead with the flame from candles. The glass cane was melted on the flame, then cooled in ashes. The name today denotes hand-cut beads that are distinguishable from factory-produced ones by their size and imperfect holes.

Industrial glass beads. These are factory-made using a mold. Usually they have a small, neat hole, but some beads also have larger holes.

Lined glass beads. These beads are made using clear glass canes whose inside hollow surface has been layered with thin gold leaf, silver leaf, or copper leaf, or lined with color.

Semi-precious stones. Trendy fashions often combine semi-precious stones with "poor" materials such as metal or glass, with good aesthetic results. The stones are usually sold as chips and include amethyst, carnelian, and quartz.

Amber beads. Amber is a fossil resin from trees that lived about 50 million years ago. Usually of a golden honey color, it is extremely light in weight.

ROUND BEADS
OPAQUE PINK

ROUND BEADS
TRANSP. CRIMSON RED

ROUND BEADS
TRANSP. SKY-BLUE

ROUND BEADS
TRANSP. GREEN IRIS

ROUND BEADS
OPAQUE YELLOW

ROUND BEADS
OPAQUE VERMILION

ROUND BEADS
OPAQUE DARK RED

ROUND BEADS
TRANSP. LIGHT TOPAZ

ROUND BEADS
OPAQUE LIGHT GREEN

ROUND BEADS
TRANSP. ORANGE

ROUND BEADS
SATIN GREEN

ROUND BEADS
TRANSP. TOPAZ

ROUND BEADS
TRANSP. GARNET

ROUND BEADS
SATIN MULTI-COLOR

ROUND BEADS
TRANSP. AMETHYST

ROUND BEADS
OPAQUE TURQUOISE

ROUND BEADS
TRANSP. GREEN

ROUND BEADS
OPAQUE BLUE

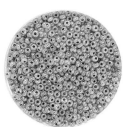

ROUND BEADS
TRANSP. ASH-BLUE

ROUND BEADS
TRANSP. GRAY

ROUND BEADS
TRANSP. DARK GRAY

ROUND BEADS
TRANSP. WHITE

ROUND BEADS
TRANSP. DARK GREEN

ROUND BEADS
TRANSP. DARK ASH

ROUND BEADS
TRANSP. DARK YELLOW

2-CUT BEADS
TRANSP. ANTIQUE WHITE

2-CUT BEADS
TRANSP. STRAWBERRY

2-CUT BEADS
TRANSP. FUCHSIA

2-CUT BEADS
TRANSP. SALMON

2-CUT BEADS
TRANSP. YELLOW

2-CUT BEADS
TRANSP. BROWN

2-CUT BEADS
TRANSP. ORANGE

2-CUT BEADS
TRANSP. BI-COLOR PURPLE

2-CUT BEADS
TRANSP. LIGHT GREEN

2-CUT BEADS
TRANSP. DARK PINK

2-CUT BEADS
TRANSP. BLUE-GRAY

2-CUT BEADS
TRANSP. AMETHYST

2-CUT BEADS
TRANSP. BI-COLOR GREEN

2-CUT BEADS
TRANSP. GREEN

2-CUT BEADS TRANSP.
BI-COLOR AMETHYST

2-CUT BEADS TRANSP.
BI-COLOR LIGHT GREEN

2-CUT BEADS
TRANSP. MINK

3-CUT BEADS
TRANSP. LIGHT TOPAZ

3-CUT BEADS
TRANSP. BLUE

3-CUT BEADS
TRANSP. RED

3-CUT BEADS
TRANSP. BLACK

3-CUT BEADS
TRANSP. DARK TOPAZ

BUGLE BEADS
SATIN BEIGE

BUGLE BEADS
TRANSP. TURQUOISE

BUGLE BEADS
TRANSP. GREEN IRIS

BUGLE BEADS
TRANSP. LILAC IRIS

BUGLE BEADS
SATIN BLACK

BUGLE BEADS
TRANSP. RED

BUGLE BEADS
TRANSP. BLUE IRIS

BUGLE BEADS
OPAQUE BLACK

BUGLE BEADS
TRANSP. BEIGE

HALF-CRYSTALS
TRANSP.

HALF-CRYSTALS
TRANSP. GOLD-ROSE

HALF-CRYSTALS
TRANSP. CRIMSON RED

HALF-CRYSTALS
SATIN BLUE

HALF-CRYSTALS
TRANSP. GRAY

HALF-CRYSTALS
TRANSP. GREEN

HALF-CRYSTALS
TRANSP. TOPAZ

HALF-CRYSTALS
TRANSP. SEA-BLUE

HALF-CRYSTALS
SATIN BLACK

HALF-CRYSTALS
TRANSP. RED

HALF-CRYSTALS
TRANSP. BROWN

HALF-CRYSTALS
TRANSP. AMETHYST

HALF-CRYSTALS
TRANSP. CERULEAN BLUE

HALF-CRYSTALS
TRANSP. GREEN IRIS

HALF-CRYSTALS
SATIN BLUE

QUARTZ CRYSTALS

HALF-CRYSTALS
TRANSP. GRAY

HALF-CRYSTALS
TRANSP. TURQUOISE

HALF-CRYSTALS
TRANSP. GRAY

LAMPWORK BEADS
TRANSP. WHITE

LAMPWORK BEADS
TRANSP. SKY-BLUE

LAMPWORK BEADS
TRANSP. BURNT UMBER

GLASS BEADS
OPAQUE ACID-TREATED

GLASS BEADS
TRANSP. DARK RED

GLASS BEADS
TRANSP. LIGHT GREEN

GLASS BEADS
TRANSP. TOPAZ

GLASS BEADS
TRANSP. TURQUOISE

GLASS BEADS
TRANSP. LIGHT BROWN

GLASS BEADS
TRANSP. AND SATIN RED

GLASS BEADS
TRANSP. MULTI-COLOR

GLASS BEADS
TRANSP. GREEN

GLASS BEADS
OPAQUE

LAMPWORK BEADS
OPAQUE FREEFORM

LAMPWORK BEADS
TRANSP. GOLD LEAF

LAMPWORK BEADS
TRANSP. COPPER LEAF

LAMPWORK BEADS
TRANSP. SILVER LEAF

LAMPWORK BEAD
TRANSP. GOLD LEAF

SEMI-PRECIOUS
AMETHYST

SEMI-PRECIOUS
CARNELIAN

AMBER BEADS

Metal Findings

Beadwork creations call for metal accessories that are sometimes indispensable for a successful project.

Bead caps. Used as supports for large beads.

Spacers. Used to separate beads on a string. An alternative is to use metal geometric-shaped ethnic beads.

Head pins. Required for drop earrings.

Ear wires and posts. Used for making earrings. They are the parts that attach the earring to the ear lobe.

Cord ends. As the name suggests, they are set at each end of a cord.

Bead tips. They hide the knots at the ends of cords.

Cones. They hold and hide the ends of several strings together, as in the twisted choker.

Clasps. There are different types on the market: barrel, lobster-claw, toggle, and spring-ring clasps.

Jump rings. Used with some clasps and to make chains.

Crimp beads. They hold the beads securely at each end of a wire or cable and block the ends of nylon stretch strings and thread.

Bases. They are the foundation on which you create pendants, rings, or pins.

Pin backs. Needed to attach a pin to clothing.

Choosing the color of these metal findings is a matter of personal taste of course, but the findings should also harmonize with the color and style of the jewelry and the season when it is worn. For cool colors, silver is preferred, while for warm hues, gold-colored findings are best. Classical-looking pieces go well with gold metal, but for a fresh, youthful style, silver is more appropriate. Silver metal is used more often in the summer, gold in winter.

Supplies

Metal wire. You need wire in several thicknesses (or gauges), depending on the project. Wire may be made of *copper*, *brass*, or *steel,* and come coated in different colors of enamel. Although rust-proof, wire does oxidize. *Aluminum* wire is useful as support wire because it is sturdier.

Thread. Some projects call for beads to be strung on thread, which comes in natural and synthetic materials, such as cotton and polyester. *Embroidery floss* is also used to cover less valuable wire.

Twine and cord. Made of *hemp* or *cotton,* they are a good choice to use with large-hole beads.

Ribbons. Trendy jewelry increasingly uses trimmings such as *double-* *satin* ribbons that are heavy and shiny, or gossamer or changing-color *organza* ribbons.

Leatherette bands. Useful for making chokers or bracelets.

Pliers. Useful for bending and crimping metal. There are two basic types: *round-nose pliers* (round-tipped) are used to round and bend the ends of metal findings, such as the pins used to make drop earrings. *Flat-nose pliers* (flat-tipped) are used to press and seal metal findings such as crimp beads, cord ends, or bead tips.

Florist wires. Necessary for assembling flowers: they are the stiff stems to which the flowers, leaves, and tendrils are attached. Use a heavy gauge for good support.

Florist tape. Green florist tape is useful for covering the parts of the flowers and for hiding the wires.

Glue products. *Nail polish* is very useful and so is *vinyl glue.* The latter is spread with a tiny *spatula*.

Needles. Although not usually used when working with wire, needles are indispensable for stringing small seed beads on thread.

Ring-size bar. Allows you to create rings of all sizes. All you need to do is wrap the wire around the size you choose and measure.

Adhesive tape. Use it to fasten the object to the worktable as you work on a project.

Pencil. Useful to outline the design of objects that require an aluminum wire core.

Graph paper. Helps you to accurately draw the designs for your projects.

Crochet hook. Useful for working with very thin metal wires and for making delicate chains.

Craft knife. Use a sharp blade to easily cut wires.

Scissors. Needless to say, they come in handy for many projects.

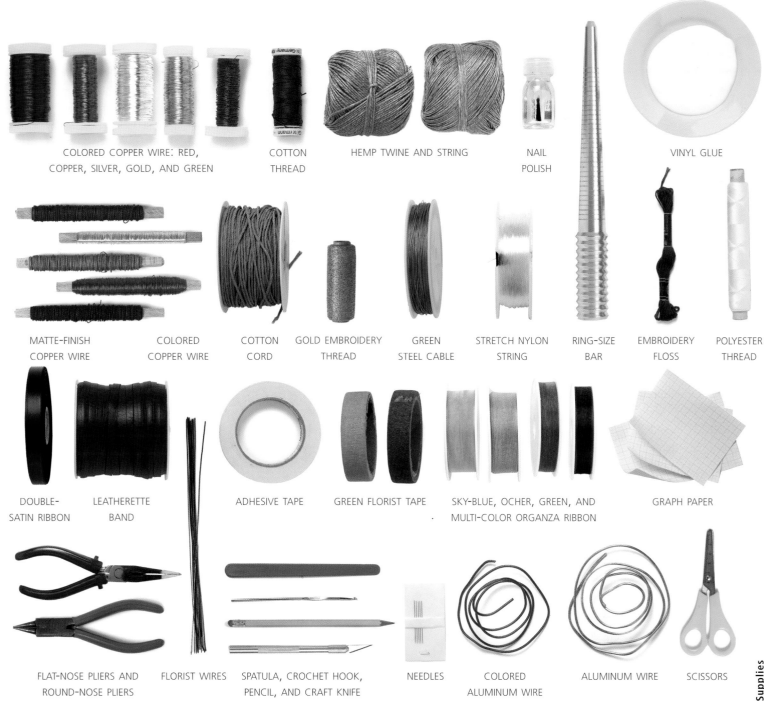

COLORED COPPER WIRE: RED, COPPER, SILVER, GOLD, AND GREEN

COTTON THREAD

HEMP TWINE AND STRING

NAIL POLISH

VINYL GLUE

MATTE-FINISH COPPER WIRE

COLORED COPPER WIRE

COTTON CORD

GOLD EMBROIDERY THREAD

GREEN STEEL CABLE

STRETCH NYLON STRING

RING-SIZE BAR

EMBROIDERY FLOSS

POLYESTER THREAD

DOUBLE-SATIN RIBBON

LEATHERETTE BAND

ADHESIVE TAPE

GREEN FLORIST TAPE

SKY-BLUE, OCHER, GREEN, AND MULTI-COLOR ORGANZA RIBBON

GRAPH PAPER

FLAT-NOSE PLIERS AND ROUND-NOSE PLIERS

FLORIST WIRES

SPATULA, CROCHET HOOK, PENCIL, AND CRAFT KNIFE

NEEDLES

COLORED ALUMINUM WIRE

ALUMINUM WIRE

SCISSORS

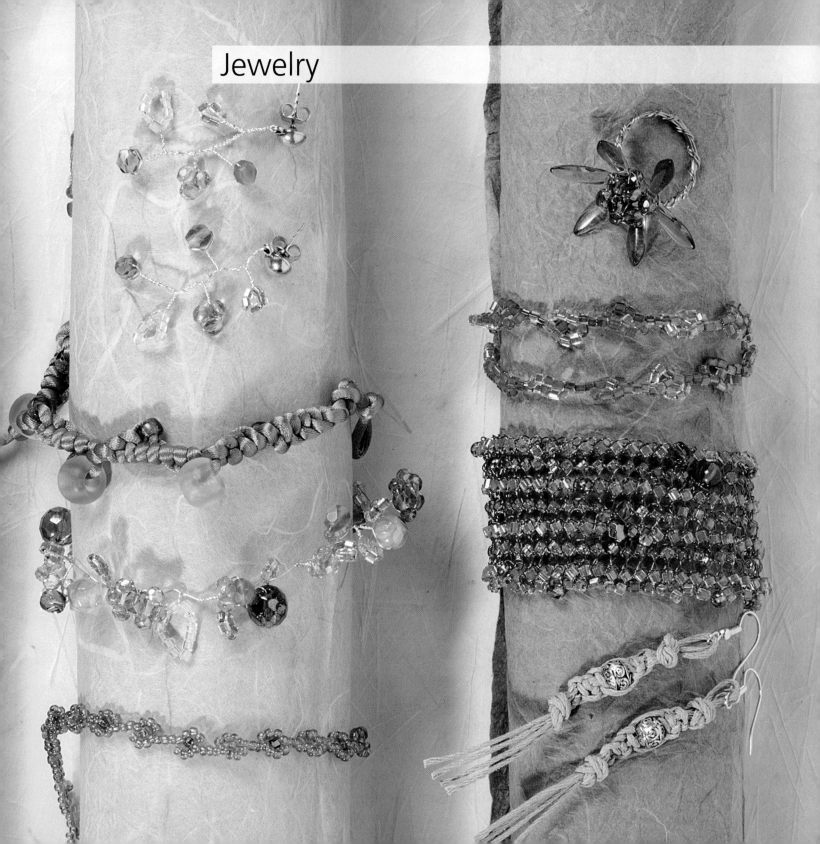

Stretch Bracelet

step by step

Time 10 MINUTES

Difficulty

Materials

10G OF TRANSP. MULTI-
COLOR GLASS BEADS (4MM)

12 IN. OF STRETCH
NYLON STRING

1 CRIMP BEAD

FLAT-NOSE
PLIERS

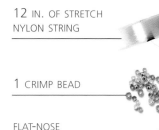

2 Once you have the desired length, insert one end of the string into a crimp bead; then insert the other end of the string in the other side of the crimp bead.

Hint

If you are working with large beads, as in this project, use a thicker string to provide better support.

3 Holding the two ends of the nylon string and the crimp bead with your fingers, slide the bracelet on your wrist and check the length.

1 Thread the beads on the nylon string, arranging the colors as you like.

4 Once you have short-ened or lengthened the bracelet according to the size you want, crimp the crimp bead with the pliers and cut the excess string. Your bracelet is now ready to wear!

Suggestion

By varying shapes and colors, you'll be able to create end-less variations with crystal beads, satin glass beads, or small seed beads. The illustration on the right gives you an idea of the possibilities.

Satellite Choker

step by step

Time 30 MINUTES

Difficulty

Materials

3 LAMPWORK BEADS WITH A FLOWER MOTIF (2CM)

18 IN. OF 12-GAUGE GREEN STAINLESS-STEEL CABLE

8 CRIMP BEADS

1 LOBSTER-CLAW CLASP

FLAT-NOSE PLIERS

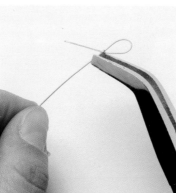

1 Insert one end of the cable into a crimp bead. Bend the end of the cable and thread it again through the crimp bead to form a ¼-inch loop. Press the crimp bead to secure the loop.

2 Starting from the opposite end of the cable, add one crimp bead followed by one lampwork bead, then another crimp bead; continue until you have used all three beads, ending with a crimp bead.

3 Fold the cable in half to find the center, then move the second lampwork bead to the center. Now slide the crimp beads to each side of the center bead and press them with the pliers. The center bead is now secured.

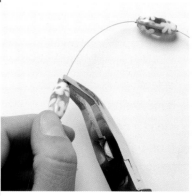

4 Follow the same procedure for the other two beads, positioning them at a distance of about 2½ inches from the central bead.

5 For the closure, string a crimp bead and a lobster-claw clasp onto the cable at the open end. Bend the end of the cable and thread it again through the crimp bead, forming a loop. Now press the crimp bead to secure the loop.

Hint

For necklaces and bracelets, use an odd number of beads so that the central bead falls in the center. Choose cables and findings in a color similar to that of the beads.

Drop Earrings

step by step

Time 30 MINUTES

Difficulty

Materials

2 TRANSP. GOLD-LEAF LAMPWORK BEADS (1.5CM)

2 GOLD HEAD PINS
2 GOLD EAR WIRES

4 TRANSP. CRIMSON RED CRYSTALS

ROUND-NOSE PLIERS

VARIATION: 2 TRANSP. WHITE LAMPWORK BEADS (1.5CM)

2 SILVER EAR WIRES
2 SILVER HEAD PINS

4 TRANSP. CRYSTALS

24-GAUGE SILVER MATTE-FINISH COPPER WIRE

1 String one crystal, one lampwork bead, and another crystal on the head pin, then cut the tip of the pin at a distance of ⅓ inch from the last crystal you strung.

2 Using your pliers, bend the end of the pin downwards, shaping it into a loop into which you will insert the ear wire.

Suggestion

You may also use these directions to make pendants. Just replace the ear wire with a small ring to attach the pendant to the necklace. Remember to use findings of the same color, in this case you would use gold.

3 For a spiral *variation* using matte-finish wire, string a crystal, a lampwork bead, and another crystal on the head pin. Cut 12 inches of wire and insert one end of it through the first crystal, then wrap it tightly twice around the pin. Now form spirals around the bead by wrapping the wire loosely around it, as in the photo at the top left of the opposite page, then fasten it to the opposite end of the pin.

4 Using your pliers, bend the upper part of the pin to form a loop, then insert the ear wire in it.

Hint

The crystal at the bottom of the earring is both decorative and functional: it prevents the bead from falling off the pin, whose head is smaller than the hole of the bead. Feel free to improvise, starting from the suggestions depicted here. For example, try setting the lampwork bead between fancy bead caps instead of crystals.

Cylinder Ring

step by step

Time 30 MINUTES

Difficulty

Materials

5G OF TRANSP. SKY-BLUE ROUND SEED BEADS

20 IN. OF POLYESTER THREAD

NEEDLE

1 CRIMP BEAD

FLAT-NOSE PLIERS

VARIATION: 5G OF OPAQUE BEIGE ROUND SEED BEADS

10 TRANSP. GOLD-ROSE CRYSTALS

1 With the needle, thread one crimp bead on the polyester string: this will secure the ring. Then add an odd number of seed beads for the desired length. With the needle, thread the polyester thread back into the crimp bead, forming a ring.

2 Using your pliers and holding the two ends of the string taut, flatten the crimp bead, thus forming the first circle from which you will start the second.

3 Add the beads one at a time: before threading the next one, always go through the hole of an even-numbered bead from the first circle (starting with the second), until you have threaded through all the even-numbered beads, forming the second circle.

4 Make more circles, always remembering to thread the needle back through the bead from the preceding circle, in an alternating order, i.e. by skipping beads. Thus, for the third circle you will thread the needle back into the odd-numbered beads, for the fourth circle, the even-numbered beads, and so on.

5 For a *variation*, thread four beads, go back into the first base bead and pull the thread until you have a clover shape. Skip three base beads and repeat the same steps around the entire circle.

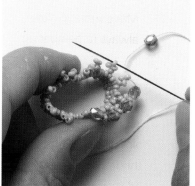

6 Finish the ring with a circle of tiny crystals that you will block by reentering with needle and thread through the top bead of each clover. Block the string by threading it through several beads, thus hiding it and reinforcing the ring.

Multi-Strand Twisted Choker

step by step

Time 4 HOURS

Difficulty

Materials

150G OF TRANSP. LIGHT TOPAZ SEED BEADS

FLAT-NOSE PLIERS

ROUND-NOSE PLIERS

80 FT. OF POLYESTER THREAD

2 GOLD HEAD PINS

2 GOLD BEAD CAPS

1 GOLD BARREL CLASP

CLEAR NAIL POLISH

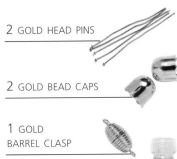

1 Prepare 48 strings of 20 inches each and thread the beads, leaving 2 inches on each side of the strings. With the round-nose pliers, bend the tip of a head pin to make a hook. Do the same with the second pin.

2 Tie the strings together at each end, making one knot at each end. Attach one knot to a head pin hook and close the hook into a small loop with the flat-nose pliers. Repeat with the other knot.

3 Cut the excess strings, leaving only ¼-inch tails, and set the knots with a drop of nail polish. Cover each knot with a bead cap, sliding the head pin through the bead cap opening.

4 Using the round-nose pliers, cut the excess from both pins, leaving only ⅓ inch showing. Then bend the ends to form a small hook to secure the bead cap and to receive the barrel clasp.

5 Insert the small rings at each side of the barrel clasp into the small head pin hooks, and with the pliers, close the hooks into small rings.

Suggestion

You may experiment using glass beads of different sizes, inserted at irregular intervals as illustrated in the blue choker at right.

Cloud Necklace

step by step

Time 1 HOUR

Difficulty

Materials

45 TRANSP. DARK RED GLASS BEADS (7MM)

45 TRANSP. DARK RED GLASS BEADS (8MM)

15 FT. OF 28-GAUGE SILVER-COLORED COPPER WIRE

FLAT-NOSE PLIERS

ROUND-NOSE PLIERS

1 Cut a 32-inch piece of the silver wire and thread 15 beads, alternating sizes. Position the first bead about 4 inches from the end by holding it with your fingers and rotating it twice. Position the second bead at a 1¼-inch distance and rotate it twice. Continue with the other beads, remembering to leave 1¼ inches between each. Leave 4 inches of empty wire at the end and cut off the excess.

2 Repeat the above step five times until you have six beaded strands of the same length. Use the flat-nose pliers to join the wires at each end, twisting them for at least 2½ inches.

3 Reinforce the ends by tightly covering them with another length of wire.

4 Use the round-nose pliers to form a hook about ½ inch from the tip of one end.

5 Take the other twisted end about 2 inches from the tip and bend it to form a loop in which you will hook the other end. Finally, reinforce the loop base with more wire.

Variation

If you use small seed beads instead of larger ones, try using them in groups of five for a nice effect.

Lariat Necklace

step by step

Time 4 HOURS

Difficulty

Materials

20G OF TRANSP. AMETHYST HEX-CUT BEADS

70 TRANSP. AMETHYST CRYSTALS

20 FT. OF POLYESTER THREAD

NEEDLE

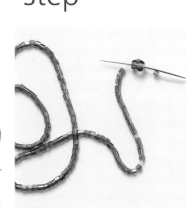

1 To make this free-form necklace, thread 5 feet of beads on the twist using the needle; leave 8 inches empty at the beginning. Next thread a crystal and a bead on the needle, then go back with the needle inside and through the crystal. This way, when you pull the thread the last bead will secure the segment. Now go back with the needle inside and through 24 beads, then pull the thread out.

2 Now thread 15 beads, one crystal, and one bead, then go back with the needle through the crystal, closing off the end. Go back with the needle through the beads of the branch you just made until you rejoin the main segment. Insert the needle through the main segment beads, counting 30, then come out with the thread and create another branch with 20 beads, one crystal, and one bead.

3 Repeat the process: go back with the needle through the crystal and the beads of the second branch until you rejoin the main segment; continue to pass through 30 beads of the main segment. Alternating the length of the branches, repeat for the entire length of the main segment. To finish this end, insert a crystal and a bead, then hide the remaining thread by going through the crystal and the beads up the branch and continue through the beads of the main segment.

4 Now finish the other end: insert a crystal and a bead in the 8-inch end from step 1. Go back with the thread through the crystal and the beads until you have used up all the 8 inches.

Suggestion

A simple lariat would make a delightful eyeglass chain. Use alternating crystals and beads, and close the ends with the appropriate clasps or hooks.

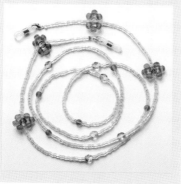

Organza Necklace

step by step

Time 1 HOUR

Difficulty

Materials

24 WIDE-HOLE GLASS BEADS AS FOLLOWS:

TRANSP. BEIGE (1CM)
SATIN GOLD (8MM)

7 FT. OF 1-IN.-WIDE BEIGE
ORGANZA RIBBON

2 GOLD CORD-ENDS

1 GOLD JUMP RING
1 GOLD LOBSTER-CLAW CLASP

FLAT-NOSE PLIERS

VARIATION: 5½ FT. OF ¾-IN.
CHANGING COLOR ORGANZA RIBBON

5 WIDE-HOLE GLASS BEADS:
TRANSP. RED AND DARK
SATIN RED (1CM)

1 Thread six beads on the ribbon, alternating the colors. Leave 5 inches at one end of the ribbon and make a double knot. Slide the first bead up to the knot and secure it with another double knot.

2 Proceed in the same manner, spacing the beads 1¼ inches apart, then cut the ribbon leaving 5 inches empty at the other end.

3 Make three more ribbons in the same way, varying the spacing of the beads, up to 2 inches apart, so that the length of the ribbons will also vary slightly.

4 Gather the ends of the four ribbons and insert a cord end at each extremity, crimping it with the flat-nose pliers.

Variation

Fold the organza ribbon twice to make four ribbons. Leaving 3 inches per side, insert the beads in the ribbons, spacing them 2½ inches apart. Secure with a knot on each side.

Hint

To join ribbons of different widths, fold the end of the wider ribbon around the thinner one, then block them with a few stitches, hiding them with a bead.

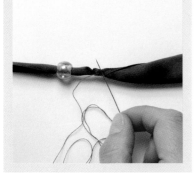

Bead and Cord Necklace

Time 2 HOURS

Difficulty

Materials

49 MIXED LAMPWORK
BEADS (4MM)

15 FT. OF
HEMP TWINE

THIN
HEMP STRING

CLEAR
NAIL POLISH

1 Cut 26 inches of hemp twine and make a double knot 6 inches from one end. String the first bead and secure it on the opposite side with another double knot. Continue to thread five more beads, spacing them 2 inches apart. Leave 6 inches of empty twine at the other end and cut the excess. Make seven more strands using the same technique and cut the end of the strands with a sharp cut so they are all exactly the same length.

2 Cut a 6-inch segment of string and thread a bead to the center. Bend the segment into a U shape around the strands, gathering the ends of the eight strands firmly in one hand. With the other hand, grasp the bead.

3 Rotate the bead so that the string is wrapped around the eight strands. At 4 inches from the end, tie a thin string of twine with a double knot and wrap it tightly around all the strands until you reach the end bead.

4 Finish with a double knot and apply a drop of nail polish to the two knots, then cut the excess thin string. To make the closing loop on the opposite end, hold the eight strands together tightly and tie a 6-inch thin string around them with a double knot, 4 inches from the strands' end. Then wrap it tightly along the 4 inches to the end.

5 Bend the end to make a loop large enough for the end bead, and reinforce the loop's base by tying a thin string around it. Make several double knots and cut the excess.

Suggestion

You could use hemp twine or string to rejuvenate your old necklaces: you will be pleasantly surprised by the results!

Jeweled Clip

step by step

Time 1 HOUR AND 30 MINUTES

Difficulty

Materials

16 SATIN BLACK CRYSTALS

1 LARGER SATIN BLACK CRYSTAL

1 ROUND PIN BASE
1 ROUND PERFORATED MOUNTING SCREEN

32 IN. OF STRETCH NYLON STRING

FLAT-NOSE PLIERS

1 Thread 10 crystals on the nylon string. Make a loop by tying the ends of the thread, then pass them through one of the holes near the edge of the mounting screen to the opposite side.

2 To block the ring to the screen, grasp one of the string ends and pass it back through another hole near the edge of the screen, trying to come up between two crystals. Now pass the string again to the back of the screen, passing over the string connecting the two crystals and pull. Continue passing the string back and front in this way until you have secured the entire circle of beads.

3 Finish by tying the ends of the string in the back of the screen. Now make a smaller circle with six crystals and place it inside the larger ring, securing it with the same technique.

4 Cut 4 inches of string, insert the large crystal, set it in the center of the rings, and tie it in the back. Finally, fasten the mounting screen to the base by crimping the fasteners in place.

Suggestion

With this technique you can create pins, rings, and earrings, using the appropriate bases. If your beads are considerably smaller or larger, adapt their quantities accordingly. Measure the mounting screen, and use a sufficient number of beads to make a circle that covers the entire surface of the base.

Crystal Crosses

step by step

Time 1 HOUR

Difficulty

Materials

30 TRANSP. GOLD-ROSE CRYSTALS

7 TRANSP. BROWN 2-CUT BEADS

20 IN. OF 24-GAUGE BRASS WIRE

1 Thread five beads on the brass wire and arrange them in the center. Close them together to make a loop, twisting the wire at the base. Thread one crystal on both wires up to the ring. Then thread two crystals on each strand of wire.

2 Repeat the procedure, first threading one crystal on the joined wires, then two crystals on each wire. End with another crystal on the joined wires.

3 Thread three crystals on one of the wires, then go back with the wire through the hole of the last central crystal in step 2 and continue to go through the crystals coming out of the second central crystal.

4 Do the same for the other wire, which together with the first will form the core of the first arm. Thread one crystal on the two joined wires, then two crystals on each wire. Thread one more crystal on the joined wires and one bead on one of the wires. Then go back with both wires through the crystals up the entire arm, coming out at the opposite end of the central body, where you will make the second arm like the first.

5 After you have completed the second arm by threading one bead, thread the wires back through the holes of the crystals. Continue through the central body, until you have hidden all the wires inside the cross.

Variations

Many variations are possible using this technique. By changing the type of beads, you can create unusual crosses depending on the facets and size of the beads. The sky-blue cross was made with the above technique, except that the beads were threaded without making ring shapes. The larger crosses require two crystals instead of one.

Macramé Necklace

step by step

Time 1 HOUR AND 30 MINUTES

Difficulty

Materials

20 FT. OF THIN HEMP STRING

2 ETHNIC METAL BEADS (7MM)

2 BALL SPACERS (7MM)

2 BALL SPACERS (4MM)

2 SILVER CORD ENDS

1 SILVER LOBSTER-CLAW CLASP

FLAT-NOSE PLIERS

NEEDLE
ADHESIVE TAPE

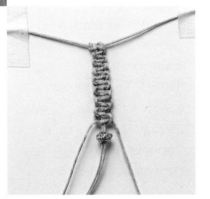

2 Bend the outside strand of the right string into a U passing under the two center strands and above the outside strand of the left string. Cross the latter over the center strands and enter the loop formed by the folded first string.

1 Using adhesive tape, tape 8 inches of hemp string to the worktable to use as support. Cut two hemp string segments of 10 feet each, fold them in half, and position them under the support string with the folded center facing up. Pass the ends of the first string through the loop, making a knot. Do the same with the second string.

3 Pull the ends of the outside strands until you have a knot. Repeat the step by bending first the outside strand of the string that's on your left, and then the one on your right. Continue alternating regularly in similar fashion.

4 Insert the decorative elements – in this case, the ball spacers and the ethnic beads, by inserting them on the two joined center strings. Then repeat the knots, inserting the decorative elements at regular distances each from the other until you have reached a length of 12 inches. Now all you need to do is make the closing. To make the loop, thread the support string through a needle.

5 Insert the needle in the first knot of step 1 creating an inverted U. Now go back into the inverted U creating a loop, then go into the loop, pull the string, and repeat the step creating many loops around the U.

6 Gather the strings at the other end of the necklace into a cord end, crimp it with the pliers, cut the excess string, and attach the lobster-claw clasp. If you prefer to leave the six string ends hanging, block them with a bead and a knot each.

"Molecule" Ring

step by step

Time 1 HOUR

Difficulty

Materials

10 TRANSP. GLASS BEADS OF ASSORTED SIZES

40 IN. OF 28-GAUGE ORANGE-COLORED COPPER WIRE

RING-SIZE BAR

FLAT-NOSE PLIERS

1 Wrap the copper wire four times around the ring-size bar at the notch for the size you need. Pull the wire taut between rounds. This is the ring on which you will set the beads according to your personal taste.

2 Block one end of the ring wire by making a small hook with the pliers and hook it to the ring. Wrap the other end around the entire ring back to the beginning.

4 Set each subsequent bead by inserting the wire back through the hole of the preceding bead.

3 Slide one bead at a time on the wire, alternating sizes, and set them by wrapping the wire around the ring.

5 Once you have reached the desired shape, wrap the remaining wire twice all around the ring. Set it by securing the end with the pliers.

Variations

Look at the photo on the right for suggestions of other possible designs. If you want, you could leave the wire loose between each bead, creating spirals.

Sea-Urchin Pendant

Time 2 HOURS AND 30 MINUTES

Difficulty

Materials

FOR THE PENDANT:
145 SMALL AMBER STONES

13 FT. OF
28-GAUGE
BRASS WIRE

VARIATION 10G OF TRANSP. RED
3-CUT BEADS

FOR THE PIN
10G OF TRANSP. DARK PINK
2-CUT BEADS

GOLD PIN BACK

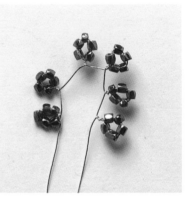

1 Thread six amber stones on the brass wire, leaving 2 inches empty at the beginning. Twist the first stone around itself twice to block it, then leave ½ inch and do the same for the second stone, and so forth.

2 Wrap the six-stone wire around itself at the base, creating a core around which you will add the remaining stones one by one, twisting each twice around itself at the base and then once around the preceding stone to secure it.

3 After inserting all the stones, finish the pendant by leaving 8 inches of wire empty to make a loop around which you will wrap the remaining wire.

1 For a *variation* using 3-cut beads, replace each amber stone with five beads, pull them into a loop and twist by wrapping the wire around itself at the base of the ring. Proceed in the same way until you have a first group of six small rings each ½ inch apart.

2 Follow the same step as for the stones, twisting the wire with the six rings around itself, creating a core around which you will add more rounds of six rings each.

Sea-Urchin Pin

Follow the same technique to make a pin. In this case, use 2-cut beads. To finish the pin, attach the pin back to the back with brass wire.

Sea-Urchin Ring

step by step

Time 1 HOUR AND 30 MINUTES

Difficulty

Materials

10G OF OPAQUE TURQUOISE
ROUND SEED BEADS

10 FT. OF 28-GAUGE SILVER-
COLORED COPPER WIRE

RING-SIZE
BAR

VARIATION:
45 QUARTZ CRYSTALS

5 TRANSP. GRAY
ACID-TREATED SMALL
GLASS BEADS

FLAT-NOSE
PLIERS

1 Wrap the silver wire five times around the ring-size bar at the notch for the size you need. Pull the wire taut between rounds. Make a hook at one end of the wire using the pliers and wrap the other end in a wide spiral all around the ring.

2 Thread 35 beads, five at a time; for each group of five form a tight circle and secure it by twisting the wire at the base around itself. Leave ¼ inch between each five-bead group.

3 Create a core: wrap the seven groups of five beads around themselves, then wrap them once around the ring to block it. Add more groups of five beads, setting each one around the preceding one by wrapping it once, until you have the desired size. End by wrapping the remaining wire several times around the ring.

Variations

You can create the same ring by replacing each group of five beads with one rock crystal.

For yet another variation, follow the same procedure but use a few beads of a different color and size. For the ring pictured below, we chose contrasting gray beads, but the photo on the right shows more ideas.

String Tie

step by step

Time 3 HOURS

Difficulty

Materials

FOR THE KNOT: 322 TRANSP. GRAY CRYSTALS

10G OF TRANSP. GRAY ROUND SEED BEADS

60 FT. OF POLYESTER THREAD

NEEDLES

6 CRIMP BEADS

FLAT-NOSE PLIERS

FOR THE NECKLACE: 50G OF TRANSP. GRAY ROUND SEED BEADS

2 SILVER HEAD PINS

1 To make the tie's "knot" cut a 10-foot piece of thread. Start by threading a crimp bead on one end. With the needle, thread 21 crystals on the thread, then pass the needle through the crimp bead and crimp it with the pliers, securing this first circle.

2 To make the second circle, thread the crystals one at a time and pass the needle through the hole of a crystal from the first circle, skipping one crystal (i.e., skip the first first-circle crystal and pass the needle through the second). Then, thread a new crystal and pass the needle through the fourth first-circle crystal, and so forth.

3 Continue to make circles until you have a cylinder that's 12 crystals in height (i.e., 12 circles). Without cutting the thread, continue by threading 36 inches of beads on the thread.

4 Create a fringe by continuing with 14 crystals, alternating them with beads, and insert a crimp bead. Go back to the knot passing the needle through the fringe (skip the crimp bead) and exit from the knot.

5 Block the crimp bead with the pliers. Make four more strands using the same procedure. To finish, make five strands of seed beads, as per steps 1 and 2 on page 32. Finish by anchoring the strands' hooks to the top of the knot.

Blooming Necklace

step by step

Time 40 MINUTES

Difficulty

Materials

8G OF TRANSP. LIGHT GREEN 2-CUT BEADS

8G OF TRANSP. FUCHSIA 2-CUT BEADS

5 TRANSP. LIGHT GREEN IRIS CRYSTALS

25 TRANSP. GREEN CRYSTALS

21 TRANSP. BROWN CRYSTALS

15 TRANSP. AMETHYST CRYSTALS

1 SILVER LOBSTER-CLAW CLASP
5 FT. OF 28-GAUGE SILVER-COLORED COPPER WIRE

FOR THE EARRINGS:
2 SILVER EAR POSTS

1 Thread crystals of different sizes and colors on 5 feet of silver-colored wire, alternating them with beads and harmonizing the colors to suit your taste. Be careful in choosing the arrangement because the beads and crystals will form a flower. In the following steps, we explain how to create a few of the many possible shapes.

2 To make a pistil, form a circle with three small yellow crystals and twist it at the base for ⅔ inch.

3 Make a flower by inserting one crystal then three smaller ones, then go back with the wire in the opposite direction through the first crystal's hole, forming a circle with the three small crystals.

4 Complete the flower by adding three small crystals, then go back with the wire in the opposite direction through the central crystal and twist the wire at the base a few times.

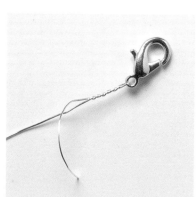

5 To make the closing, insert a lobster-claw clasp at one end of the wire and twist the base for ¾ inch. At the other end of the wire make a loop for attaching the clasp by bending the wire's tip in a ring shape and twisting it to the base.

Earrings

Place an amethyst crystal in the center of a 20-inch wire and set it by twisting the wire at the base for ¼ inch. Insert nine beads at one end and three crystals at the other. Form one circle with the beads and another one with the crystals; twist each base for at least ¼ inch. Continue, alternating shapes and colors. Close the earring by twisting the two ends of the wire together and attaching an ear post.

Crocheted Earrings

step by step

Time 1 HOUR

Difficulty

Materials

10G OF TRANSP. DARK GRAY ROUND SEED BEADS

15 FT. OF 28-GAUGE SILVER-COLORED COPPER WIRE

1 No. 1.75 CROCHET HOOK

2 SILVER EAR WIRES

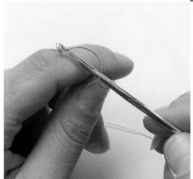

1 Thread all the beads on the wire, leaving 2 inches of wire empty, then form a circle. Insert the crochet hook in the circle and make a very small stitch: place the wire on the hook and bring a bead to the same position, hook the bead and slide it into the first circle, sliding it past the hook's tip, thus creating the first stitch. Now a new circle is on the hook. Create three more stitches following the same procedure.

2 Close this round: insert the crochet hook into the first stitch, hook the wire, place it on the hook together with a bead, and slide it inside the two circles that are on the hook.

3 Now work two stitches for each base point. Insert the crochet hook in one base circle and create a stitch by hooking the wire and a bead. Repeat using the same base circle until you have a "doily" with 13 stitches.

4 Now cast off. Insert the crochet hook in a stitch from the last circle, then add the next stitch – now you have three circles on your hook. Hook the wire with the beads, place it on the hook together with one bead, and slide it into the three circles, creating a new stitch. Continue in the same way, closing two stitches together until you have only one final stitch that you will unthread from the hook.

5 Attach the ear wire to the "ball" you have created by wrapping the wire several times inside the last stitch, then bury the wire tip inside the earring.

Variation

An interesting variation to the above technique is the "doily," which you can create by simply eliminating the stitch-reduction step.

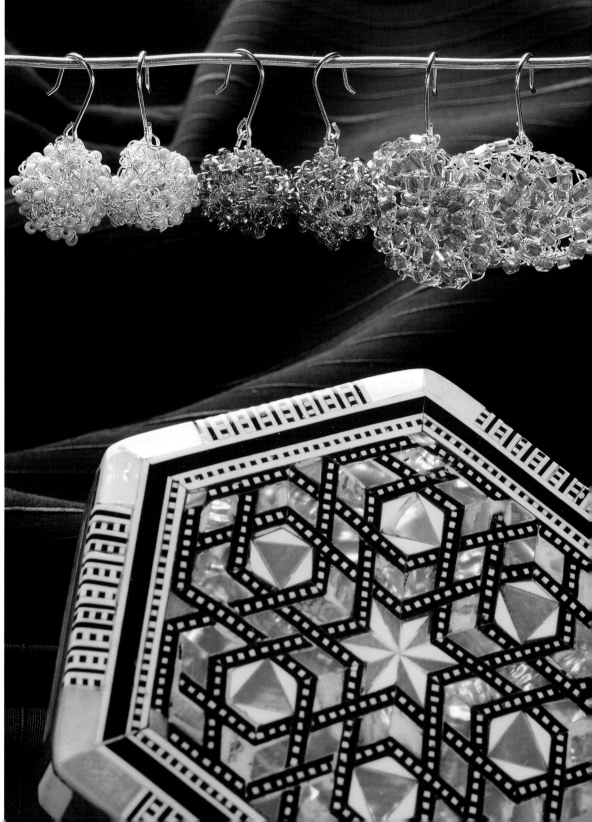

Crocheted Bracelet

step by step

Time 1 HOUR

Difficulty

Materials

15G OF TRANSP. BROWN 2-CUT BEADS

30 FT. OF 28-GAUGE BRASS WIRE

1 No. 3 CROCHET HOOK

1 SILVER SPRING-RING CLASP

ROUND-NOSE PLIERS

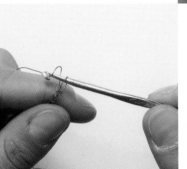

1 Thread all the beads on the wire, leaving 2 inches of wire empty; then form a circle and insert the crochet hook in the circle. Place the wire on the hook and bring a bead to the same position. Hook the bead and slide it into the first circle, creating the first stitch. Make sure you keep the stitch small. Follow the same procedure to make a chain of 45 stitches, using one bead for each stitch.

2 To make the second chain, insert the crochet hook in the next-to-last chain, then take the wire, lay it on top of the hook with one bead, and slide it inside the two circles that are on the hook.

3 Make five more chains. To block the chains, leave 6 inches of wire empty and cut the excess. Slide the 6-inch segment through the last stitch and bend it into an arch shape until you slide it into the first chain, thus forming a loop.

4 If the wire loop is too thin, bend it again into an arch shape up to the end of the last stitch, go back to the first chain, and wrap the remaining wire around the loop.

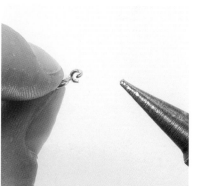

5 Attach the spring-ring clasp to the other end. With the pliers, open the small ring, rotating the metal vertically (never open it like a fan), then attach the clasp to the center of the bracelet's edge.

Choker and Ring

If you want to make a choker following the same procedure, make a chain of the same circumference as your neck, following the same steps as for the bracelet. For a ring, follow the same procedure, but remember to close it by hooking the crochet hook to the first stitch of the first chain, making a very small stitch until you reach the desired width.

Flower Choker

Time 2 HOURS AND 30 MINUTES

Difficulty

Materials

5G OF SATIN GREEN
ROUND SEED BEADS

5G OF TRANSP. CRIMSON
RED ROUND SEED BEADS

18 LARGE TRANSP.
GREEN CRYSTALS

18 SMALL TRANSP.
CRIMSON RED CRYSTALS

8 FT. OF
NYLON STRING

20 IN. OF BLACK
LEATHERETTE FLAT RIBBON

1 Cut 6 feet of nylon string and thread six green beads, placing them in the center of the string. Cross the two ends of the string through the hole of the first bead and pull to create a ring. This will be your base.

2 At one end of the string thread one green crystal, two red beads, one red crystal, two red beads, and one green crystal. Skipping one green base bead, thread the string through the next base bead, making the first small arch.

3 Make two more arches, each time skipping one base bead. Complete the outside circle by crossing the string through the hole of the first green base bead. Go back inside the corresponding green crystal and pull the string out.

4 To complete the outside red crown, thread two red beads, one red crystal, and two more red beads. Thread the nylon string through the first red arch, thus making a connecting arch. Do the same for the other two spaces, until you have closed the red crown. Prepare the flower for the last step: thread the string out of a red crystal and thread the other end of the string, unused until now, into the opposite side of the crown.

5 Thread six green beads on each end of the string, making two loops that you will attach to the flat flower by going back with the string through the holes of the inside crystals. Tie the ends of the string together and cut the excess. Make two more flowers using the same procedure. Then take the leatherette ribbon and slide it through the green loops, arranging the flowers along the ribbon. Of course, you can make more flowers if you so desire.

Crystal Bracelet and Ring

step by step

Bracelet

Time 2 HOURS AND 30 MINUTES

Difficulty

Materials

 10G OF TRANSP. TOPAZ ROUND SEED BEADS

40 TRANSP. BROWN CRYSTALS

40 TRANSP. ORANGE CRYSTALS

5 FT. OF NYLON STRING

10 SMALL GOLD JUMP RINGS

1 GOLD LOBSTER-CLAW CLASP

FLAT-NOSE PLIERS

2 Continue by threading one orange crystal, one topaz bead, and one brown crystal in each end of the string. Add one more bead and cross the ends of the string into this last bead, pulling taut.

1 Cut 5 feet of nylon string and thread one orange crystal, six topaz beads, one more orange crystal, and one more topaz bead. Cross the two ends of the string through the hole of the last bead and pull, creating a ring in the center of the string, as pictured above, with the last bead in the center.

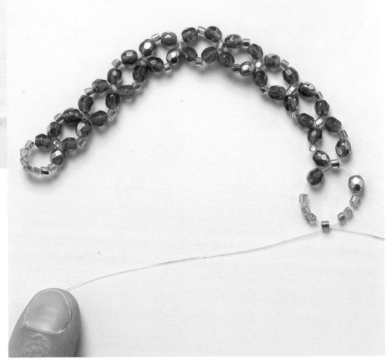

3 Alternate the color of the crystals to make a clover design of different colors. Once you have reached the size of your wrist, insert three beads at each end of the string, plus one more bead through which you will cross the ends of the string.

5 String one orange crystal on the end of the inside string, then pass the string through the bead connecting the last two clovers. String one brown crystal and one bead on the end of the outside string. Cross both ends into this last bead.

4 Now move to the edge of the bracelet: with the right end of the string go back through the holes of the last two beads of the last arch. With the left end of the string, go back through the holes of the remaining beads on the arch, going in the opposite direction and crossing the other end in the second bead. On the end of the inner string, thread five beads, one orange crystal, and one bead. On the end of the outer string, string one bead and one orange crystal, then cross both ends inside the last bead you inserted.

6 Continue in similar fashion until you reach the end of the bracelet. String one crystal on each end of the string, thread the end of the inside string through a base bead, and always end with one bead into which you cross both ends.

7 Once you reach the opposite end of the bracelet, insert the end of the inside string through the second bead of the initial loop, then string one bead through which you will again cross the ends of the string. Finally, thread one brown crystal and four beads on the outside string.

8 Finish by passing the string back through the holes of all the bracelet beads. Finally, use the pliers to attach the clasp to one end of the bracelet and a ring to the other end. Finish by inserting the rings into one another until you have a small chain.

Ring

Time 1 HOUR

Difficulty

Materials

3G OF TRANSP. AMETHYST ROUND SEED BEADS

16 TRANSP. AMETHYST CRYSTALS

12 TRANSP. LIGHT PINK CRYSTALS

18 TRANSP. GREEN CRYSTALS

32 IN. OF NYLON STRING

step by step

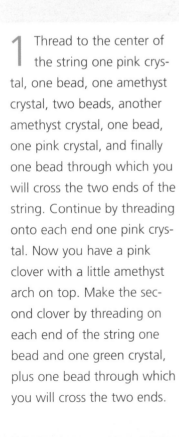

1 Thread to the center of the string one pink crystal, one bead, one amethyst crystal, two beads, another amethyst crystal, one bead, one pink crystal, and finally one bead through which you will cross the two ends of the string. Continue by threading onto each end one pink crystal. Now you have a pink clover with a little amethyst arch on top. Make the second clover by threading on each end of the string one bead and one green crystal, plus one bead through which you will cross the two ends.

2 Complete the green clover by threading on each end of the string one green crystal and one bead; then make more clovers, alternating the colors.

3 Move to one edge of the bracelet and continue in the opposite direction: on each end of the string thread one crystal, one bead, and one crystal, then go through the bead connecting the last two clovers of the bracelet and continue.

4 Once you have completed the second row, insert one bead on each end of the string and cross the ends through the hole of a crystal.

5 Continue until you reach the desired length to fit your finger.

6 Finish the ring by attaching the last row to the opposite end of the ring. To close it, thread both ends of the string several times through the holes of the crystals. For a narrow ring, stop at steps 3 or 4, and close.

Woven Bracelet

Time 4 HOURS

Difficulty

Materials

10G OF SATIN GREEN ROUND SEED BEADS

10G OF TRANSP. WHITE ROUND SEED BEADS
10G OF TRANSP. SKY-BLUE ROUND SEED BEADS

10G OF TRANSP. RED ROUND SEED BEADS
10G OF TRANSP. LIGHT TOPAZ ROUND SEED BEADS

30 FT. OF POLYESTER THREAD

FLAT-NOSE PLIERS
ADHESIVE TAPE

2 SILVER CORD ENDS
16 SMALL SILVER JUMP RINGS

1 SILVER LOBSTER-CLAW CLASP
NEEDLE
CRAFT KNIFE

1 14x16-IN. PIECE OF
CARDBOARD, SCISSORS

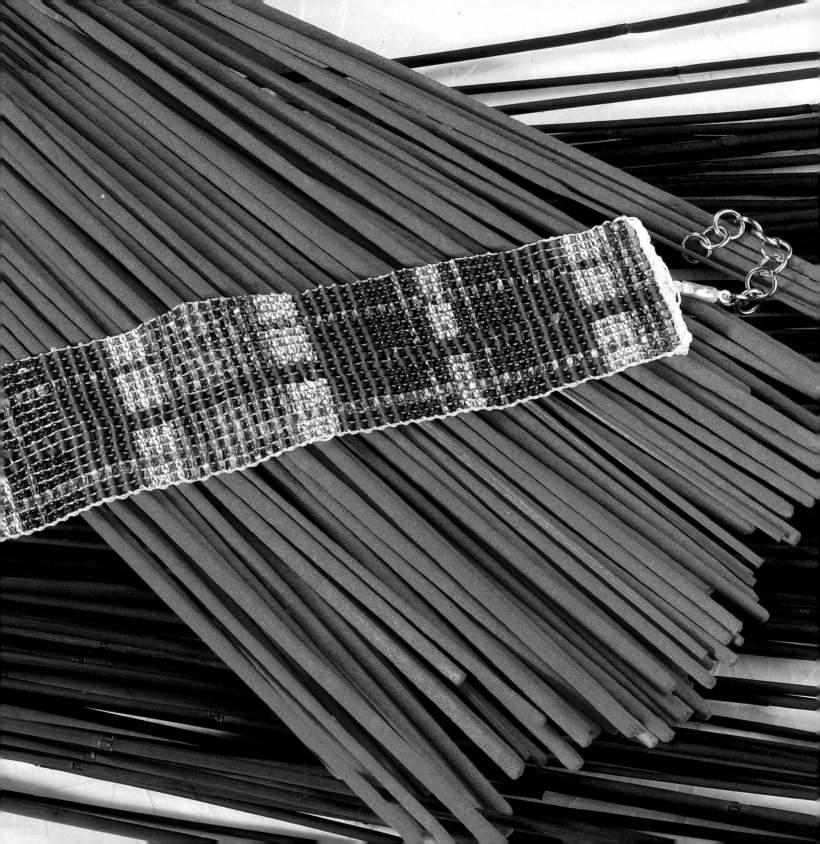

step by step

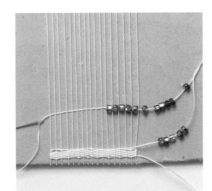

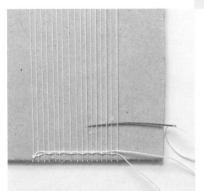

2 Working from right to left, thread the beads following the pattern on page 71. Slide the beads under all the vertical threads, placing one bead in each space.

1 Prepare the loom by fastening one end of the polyester thread to the cardboard with adhesive tape and winding the twist around the cardboard at regular intervals until you have 16 vertical spaces. Now block the end of the string with more adhesive tape. Take a 40-inch segment of thread, thread it on a needle and attach it to the loom by sliding it under all the odd-numbered vertical support threads (the warp). Repeat this last step five times.

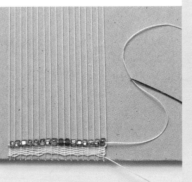

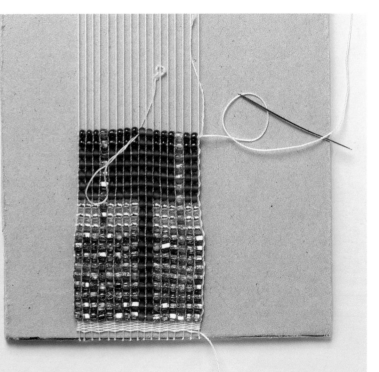

3 Go back with the needle through the hole of each bead, making sure that the return thread is on top of the vertical threads; otherwise the beads will not be attached to the warp.

4 If you find that you need more thread, slide the new thread under the beads by going back through the holes of the last row and continue.

5 Once you have finished weaving, turn the cardboard over and cut the vertical threads in the center; weave the ends together on each side of the bracelet, insert them into the cord ends, and crimp with the pliers to block.

6 Finish the back of the bracelet by cutting off the excess, if any, from the added thread segments.

7 Finally, using the pliers attach the rings to one cord end to make a small chain. Attach the clasp to the other cord end.

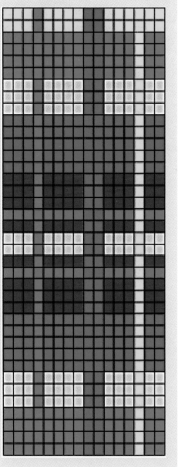

"Grid" Pendant

step by step

Time 1 HOUR AND 20 MINUTES

Difficulty

Materials

6 TRANSP. WHITE LAMPWORK BEADS

1 MOTHER-OF-PEARL BUTTON

5 FT. OF 28-GAUGE GRAY MATTE-FINISH COPPER WIRE

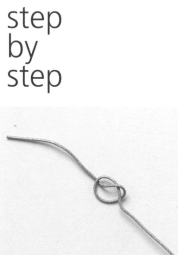

1 Leaving the first 1¼ inches of wire empty, make a wide knot in which you will insert the opposite end of the wire to form a loop.

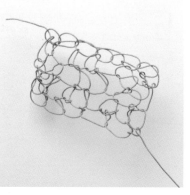

2 Insert the wire into the loop again to make a second loop (the beads will hide any imperfections). Continue until you have a 2-inch chain of loops.

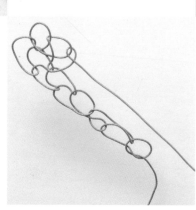

3 Now insert the wire in the next-to-last loop, thus moving to the side of the chain. Continue by first hooking the last loop you made, then the loop from the first chain, and so on down the line.

4 Continue weaving a net of interlocking loops until you have a rectangle measuring 2 by 1 inches.

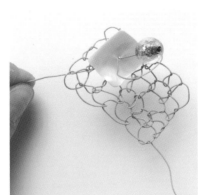

5 Thread the mother-of-pearl button and one lampwork bead on the wire. Pass the end of the wire back into the button-hole and continue to decorate the pendant with beads in assorted colors and shapes according to your taste. Finish by winding the 1¼ inches of initial empty wire end from step 1 around the grid's perimeter. With the remaining wire from the opposite end, make a loop for attaching the pendant to the necklace and wind the excess wire around it.

Variation

Increasing or decreasing the number of loops will result in different pendants. To make a round grid, hook the first loops to the initial loop and build the subsequent circles with arches.

"Grid" Ring

step
by
step

Time 1 HOUR AND 20 MINUTES

Difficulty

Materials

1 WIDE-HOLE, SATIN
RED GLASS BEAD

1 WIDE-HOLE, TRANSP. DARK
RED GLASS BEAD

2 TRANSP. DARK RED
SMALLER GLASS BEADS

10 TRANSP. RED
CRYSTALS

7 FT. OF 24-GAUGE RED
MATTE-FINISH COPPER WIRE

1 RING-SIZE BAR

2 Continue in the same way, creating new loops always inside the initial loop, until you have a flower with seven petals.

1 The procedure for this ring is similar to that of the grid pendant. Make a wide knot and go back into it forming a loop.

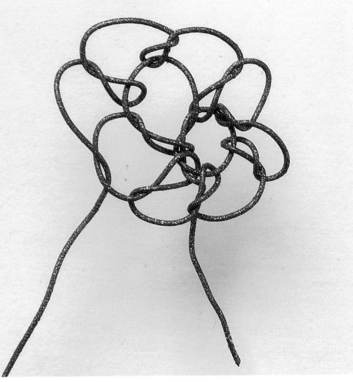

3 Continue to work in the round, making small arches between the petals of the preceding step until you have a flower about 1¼ inches in diameter.

4 Pass the wire through the center of the grid and thread a satin bead to the center, then go back with the wire inside the grid and thread the other beads. Attach each one to the base and alternate size and shape.

5 Place the flower on the ring-size bar at the notch for your ring size. Wind the remaining wire around the notch, ending after each round on the front of the ring. Secure the wires by winding them around the base of the grid.

Tassels

Time 5 HOURS

Difficulty

Materials

63 TRANSP. GREEN CRYSTALS
28 SMALL TRANSP. GREEN CRYSTALS

1 TRANSP. LIGHT GREEN
GLASS BEAD

30G OF TRANSP. GREEN IRIS
ROUND SEED BEADS, NEEDLES

8 IN. OF 28-GAUGE SILVER COPPER WIRE
20 FT. OF POLYESTER THREAD

10 FT. OF NYLON STRING
1 CRIMP BEAD, 1 SILVER HEAD PIN

ROUND-NOSE PLIERS
FLAT-NOSE PLIERS

VARIATION: 10G OF TRANSP. LILAC LONG
BUGLE BEADS, 24 AMETHYST CHIPS

20G OF TRANSP. AMETHYST ROUND SEED BEADS
20 FT. OF GRAY 28-GAUGE MATTE-
FINISH COPPER WIRE

step by step

2 Without cutting the wire, thread nine small crystals, then skip the two first crystals next to the string's exit point and thread the needle through the hole of the next crystal.

5 Knot the strings together and even out the length of the knot. Hook the head pin to it by curving the tip with the round-nose pliers. Close the hook into a circle and wrap everything with silver wire.

1 With the needle, thread seven crystals and a crimp bead on the nylon string; come back with the needle through the crimp bead and close the loop by pressing the crimp bead with the flat-nose pliers. Continue to make rounds by threading one crystal at a time. Before inserting the next one, remember to pass the needle through the hole of a crystal from the first loop, skipping one crystal, as explained on page 54. Make a cylinder four crystals wide.

3 Continue in similar fashion, pulling the string taut, until you have hooked seven lateral loops to the base cylinder, at regular intervals, i.e. always by skipping two base crystals.

4 Thread 30g of seed beads on the polyester thread, forming nine 9-inch strings, seven 7-inch strings, and five 6-inch strings. Before cutting the thread, leave at least 3 inches empty at the end of each strand.

6 To cover the knot, insert the crystal cylinder in the head pin, and finish with a lampwork bead. Close the pin hook into a circle, thus forming the loop for the tiebacks.

Amethyst Variation

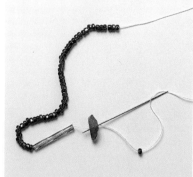

2 Hook 12 inches of matte-finish copper wire to the knot by wrapping it around the knot. Without cutting the wire, fold it to make a loop and twist it at the base.

5 Finish by inserting the amethyst ring on the matte-finish wire knot by pulling the wire loop through the top. Finally, widen the loop to secure the cylinder.

1 For the amethyst variation, prepare 21 polyester strings each 5 inches long, stringing on each one of them 2¾ inches of round seed beads, one long bugle bead, one amethyst chip, and one more seed bead. Thread the needle back through the hole of the amethyst chip, the long bugle bead, and all the seed beads, leaving only the final bead free. Knot the strings together and even out the knot length.

3 Now make the cylinder to cover the knot: thread four amethyst chips on 10 feet of nylon string and cross the ends through the hole of the last chip. Insert one chip on each string end; insert a third chip and cross the ends of the string through it.

4 Continue to follow this procedure until you have a 2-inch segment. Thread the two ends of the string through the hole of the center amethyst of the first round, making a ring; then go back with the ends of the string through the holes of the other chips, thus securing the cylinder, and make a tight knot.

Stalk of Wheat

step by step

Time 2 HOURS

Difficulty

Materials

25G OF TRANSP. LIGHT TOPAZ ROUND SEED BEADS

GOLD EMBROIDERY THREAD

25 FT. OF 28-GAUGE GOLD-COLORED COPPER WIRE

1 FLORIST WIRE

NAIL POLISH

FLAT-NOSE PLIERS

1 Take 20 inches of gold copper wire, and, leaving the first 4 inches empty, thread 2½ inches of topaz beads on it. Twist the wires at the base to form an elongated ring as shown above. Take one of the wire ends and twist it around the top of the ring. Allow the wire to move freely above the ring, measure 3 inches, and cut the excess: this is the first caryopse or spikelet with its grains and its awn pointing upward.

2 Prepare 43 more spikelets. Join them together in groups of four by twisting the wires at the base and leaving the awns free.

3 Arrange the 11 groups of four spikelets each, twisting them around the florist wire. Start at the top and move downward, arranging them around the rod to make the stalk.

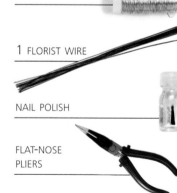

4 Cover the length of the rod with the gold embroidery thread.

5 To finish, it is a good idea to block the end of the embroidery thread with clear nail polish.

Tiny Roses

step by step

Time 1 HOUR

Difficulty

Materials

10G OF TRANSP. PINK
2-CUT BEADS

5G OF TRANSP. BI-COLOR
GREEN 2-CUT BEADS

7 FT. OF 28-GAUGE SILVER-
COLORED COPPER WIRE

20 IN. OF 28-GAUGE
GREEN-COLORED COPPER
WIRE

GREEN FLORIST
TAPE

1 Leaving the first 4 inches empty, thread three groups of beads on the silver wire: a central group with 21 beads and two lateral ones with 19 beads each. Block the bottom of each group by twisting the wire once, forming three egg-shaped rings. Leave 4 inches of wire empty and cut the excess wire.

2 Take the remaining silver wire, leave 4 inches empty, thread 11 beads, and insert the end of the wire through the center bead of each ring, alternating with three more beads. Finish with 11 more beads, leave 4 inches empty, and cut.

3 Twist the base wire of each small crown with the base of the preceding wire. Continue until you have four petals. Block them by twisting their wires together, then twist all the petal wires into one stem.

4 To make the leaf, take the green wire, leave the first 4 inches empty, and thread seven beads, leaving another 4 inches empty. Bend the wire into a loop as shown by twisting it at the base. In the second, longer wire segment, thread eight more beads and wrap the wire twice around the first, forming an oblong ring. This is the leaf's core.

5 Thread eight more beads on the same wire; twist it around the leaf base. Make another filament going up-ward, slightly longer than the leaf's core; block it by twisting it around the opposite wire end at the top of the leaf.

6 Continue with two more filaments. Finish by hid-ing the wire inside the last filament and twisting the ends around the leafstalk. Finally, attach the leaf to the flower stem and wrap every-thing with florist tape.

Daisy

step
by
step

Time 1 HOUR AND 30 MINUTES

Difficulty

Materials

40G OF TRANSP. ANTIQUE WHITE 2-CUT BEADS

5G OF TRANSP. DARK YELLOW ROUND SEED BEADS

30 FT. OF 24-GAUGE SILVER, MATTE-FINISH COPPER WIRE

40 IN. OF 24-GAUGE GOLD-COLORED COPPER WIRE

GREEN FLORIST TAPE

FLAT-NOSE PLIERS

1 FLORIST WIRE

2 Using the second end of the wire, create six more beaded filaments, gradually increasing their length. Fasten the filaments going upward to the tip of the petal and those going downward to the base, and twist to close.

1 Make a petal by following the same procedure as the rose leaf on page 84. String 21 white beads on a silver wire about 40 inches in length. Fold the wire into a loop and twist it at the base. On the other end of the wire, string a slightly larger number of white beads and wrap the wire twice around the first wire, forming an oblong beaded ring.

3 For the center button, use the gold wire: thread five yellow beads, twist the wire at the base to form a ring, then make a second ring around the first by increasing the number of beads. Fasten it to the base by twisting the wire.

4 Continue until you have a four-ring button, then go back with the wire through the last ring coming out on the opposite side but aligned with it.

5 Bring both ends of the
wire to the back center
of the button and twist
them at the base.

6 Using the pliers, attach
the daisy petals to the
florist wire, inserting the
button at the center. Attach
the leaves, and wrap the
length of the florist
wire with green
florist tape.

Iris

Time 3 HOURS

Difficulty

Materials

60G OF TRANSP. ORANGE
2-CUT BEADS

70G OF TRANSP. ANTIQUE
WHITE 2-CUT BEADS

10G OF TRANSP.
AMETHYST 3-CUT BEADS

20G OF TRANSP.
BI-COLOR GREEN
2-CUT BEADS

10 FT. OF 28-GAUGE GREEN-
COLORED COPPER WIRE

40 FT. OF 28-GAUGE SILVER-
COLORED COPPER WIRE

1 FLORIST WIRE

GREEN FLORIST TAPE

2 Fasten the last beaded filament to the petal base and hide the other strand by passing it through this last segment.

1 Take 7 feet of silver wire, leave 8 inches bare, and string seven orange beads. Leave another 4 inches bare and fold the wire in a loop, twisting it at the base. In the longer strand of wire insert eight more beads and wrap this wire twice around the other strand, forming an oblong beaded ring. Continue building filaments, following the procedure for the rose leaf on page 84, but in this case, before blocking the upward fila- ment, remember to add one bead to the short strand.

3 Follow the same proce- dure to make the outer petals. String 18 antique white beads, then add 14 filaments around it.

4 Now make the amethyst pistils. Take 12 inches of silver wire, string 14 amethyst beads, close the wire into a loop, and string five more beads on one strand of the wire. Block this second bead- ed segment by hooking its strand to the opposite end of the ring, then bring the ends of both strands to the button center, twisting them to- gether into a thin stem. This top button is called the "stigma" of the pistil.

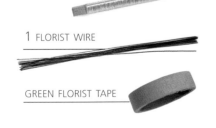

5 String 20 amethyst beads on the twisted wire stem, sliding them up to the base of the stigma. This thin stem is called the "filament" of the pistil. Prepare three more pistils and attach them all together by wrapping the twisted wire stems at the base together.

6 Prepare the leaves like the rose leaf on page 84. Use 60 green beads for the first filament, more for the other four, longer filaments. Assemble the flower on the florist wire: surround the pistils with the petals, attach the leaves, and wrap the florist wire with green tape.

Wisteria

step by step

Time 4 HOURS

Difficulty

Materials

40G OF TRANSP. BI-COLOR PURPLE 2-CUT BEADS

20G OF TRANSP. BI-COLOR GREEN 2-CUT BEADS

65 FT. OF 24-GAUGE GREEN-COLORED COPPER WIRE

GREEN FLORIST TAPE

1 FLORIST WIRE

3 Following the same procedure, make 19 three-ring petals and 11 four-ring petals. Wrap the stems of the three different petals together with insulating tape. Using all the remaining petals, follow your whim to form groups with different numbers of petals of different sizes.

2 Prepare 23 petals by adding more beaded rings to the ring of step 1, blocking each round with a twist of the wire at the base.

1 Make three pistils using 10 inches of green wire for each: slide seven purple beads to the center, close the wire into a ring by twisting the two ends of the wire at the base, and wrap the stem with insulating tape.

4 Now assemble the composition by attaching the smaller petal groups just below the pistils and the larger ones gradually further down the florist wire. Add the leaves and cover the entire stem with florist tape.

90 | **Wisteria**

5 To make the leaves, take 40 inches of wire, leave the first 6 inches bare, and string nine green beads on it. Leave 4 more inches bare and bend the wire in a loop, twisting it at the base. String 10 beads on the longer wire strand and wrap it twice at the base of the first, forming an oblong ring. Using the same longer wire strand, create seven more filaments, gradually increasing their length. Like the iris leaves on page 88, fasten the upward filaments to the top of the leaf, remembering to add one bead to the shorter strand before twisting the wire. Fasten the downward filaments of the leaf by twisting the wire to the base of the leaf. Finish by hiding the short end of the wire passing it through the beads of the last filament.

Poppy

Time 1 HOUR AND 30 MINUTES

Difficulty

Materials

15G OF OPAQUE DARK
RED ROUND SEED BEADS

10G OF TRANSP. BLACK
ROUND SEED BEADS

5G OF TRANSP. GREEN
3-CUT BEADS

20 FT. OF 28-GAUGE
RED COPPER WIRE

10 FT. OF 28-GAUGE
BLACK COPPER WIRE

10 FT. OF 28-GAUGE
GREEN COPPER WIRE

1 FLORIST WIRE
GREEN FLORIST TAPE

1 Cut a 5-foot segment of red wire and slide 31 red beads to the center. Close it into a ring by twisting the two ends of the wire at the base. Add two lateral rings of 29 beads each and fasten them to the base as well. Finally, make two more outside rings of 27 beads each. Cut a new 10-inch wire segment, thread it through the hole of the bead at the top of the last ring, add three new beads, and continue threading the wire through the top bead of each ring, alternating with three new beads in between each ring.

2 Finish this first petal by threading 16 beads on each end of this second wire segment and twisting them to the ends of the base wire. Then make three more petals using this procedure.

3 For the pistils, cut 40 inches of black wire, make six rings with 15 black beads each and cross the ends to close the crown. Cut another 40 inches of black wire and make nine rings with 13 black beads each. Close it and attach it to the first crown by twisting the ends together.

4 Make the capsule by following the procedure of the red petal. Use 40 inches of green wire: make a central ring with nine green beads and four side rings of seven green beads each, then hook a second, shorter wire to them, alternating with two new beads in between the top of each arch. Thread seven beads on each end of the second wire segment and attach each end by twisting it to the end of the base wire closest to it.

5 Finish the capsule with a black button. Take a 12-inch piece of black wire, thread three black beads on it and make a ring. Make a second ring with 13 beads, fasten it to the base with a twist, and insert the button in the capsule.

6 Twist together the ends of the capsule and the button. Now assemble the flower. Make the leaves by following the method of the iris leaves on page 88 and attach all the elements to a florist wire, covering everything with florist tape.

Zinnia

step by step

Time 2 HOURS AND 30 MINUTES

Difficulty

Materials

5G OF OPAQUE YELLOW
ROUND SEED BEADS

15G OF TRANSP. SALMON
2-CUT BEADS

15G OF SATIN GREEN
ROUND SEED BEADS

20 FT. OF 28-GAUGE SILVER-
COLORED COPPER WIRE

20 FT. OF 28-GAUGE
GREEN COPPER WIRE

GREEN FLORIST TAPE

1 FLORIST WIRE

1 Take the silver wire, leave the first 4 inches bare and string the yellow beads, making seven rings of 10 beads each. Close the rings by twisting the base. Leaving another 4 inches bare, cut the wire and twist the two strands together.

2 To make the petals, take the silver wire, leave the first 4 inches bare, and slide 10 salmon beads to the center, twisting the base of the ring. Slide three more beads on the longer strand of wire.

3 Fasten this center filament by hooking its wire to the opposite top of the ring, then bring it back to the base by going through the holes of the filament beads. Now twist both of the ends together to form a thin stem and cut the long part of the wire.

4 Following the same procedure, make seven petals, then 12 more using 16 beads for the ring and 12 more petals with 18 beads for the ring. Adapt the length of the center filaments to the size of the rings.

5 Make five leaves using, for each leaf, 12 inches of green wire threaded with 13 beads. Continue following the method outlined for the iris leaf on page 88. This done, wrap each leaf stem with florist tape.

6 Now assemble the flower: surround the pistil with the smaller petals and continue to arrange the other petals around it in order of increasing size. Attach the flower and the leaves to the florist wire and cover everything with florist tape.

Olive Tree

step by step

Time 8 HOURS

Difficulty

Materials

100G OF SATIN GREEN
ROUND SEED BEADS

65 FT. OF 28-GAUGE
GREEN COPPER WIRE

13 FT. OF 9-GAUGE
ALUMINUM WIRE

GREEN FLORIST TAPE

1 Thread all 100g of beads on the green wire, leaving 4 inches bare at the beginning, and form one eight-bead ring, twisting the wire at the base several times as shown in the photograph above. Make four more rings along the same wire, setting them at regular intervals.

2 Using the same method, make a sixth ring: this will be the central leaf of the small olive branchlet. Twist the wires at the base of this leaf leaving a bit more space, thus making a longer peduncle for it.

3 Continue to make five more rings symmetrical and opposite to the first five, wrapping the wire to the center branchlet as you go along. Following this procedure, make 86 branchlets.

4 Assemble each two branchlets into a pair, twisting the base wires together and shaping the rings to make them fuller. Now you have 43 branchlets.

5 Join the 43 branchlets in groups of three and wrap the stem of each group with insulating tape.

6 For the trunk, cut the aluminum wire in 12 12-inch segments, wrap each with tape and twist together in a classical bonsai shape. Widen the wires on top and attach branches with more tape. Finally, widen the bottom of the trunk to make a solid base.

Peach Tree

step by step

Time 7 HOURS

Difficulty

Materials

50G OF TRANSP. GREEN
IRIS ROUND SEED BEADS

130 FT. OF 28-GAUGE
GREEN COPPER WIRE

5G OF OPAQUE PINK
ROUND SEED BEADS

15G OF TRANSP. DARK
PINK ROUND SEED BEADS

GREEN FLORIST TAPE

55 FT. OF 28-GAUGE SILVER-
COLORED COPPER WIRE

1 PEACH TREE BRANCH

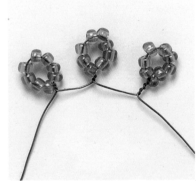

1 Cut a 20-inch segment of green wire; leave the first 4 inches bare. Following the technique on page 96, make 84 leaves, each one consisting of seven rings of eight green beads each.

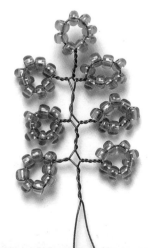

2 To make the peach tree flower, first make the pistils by threading three light pink beads to the center of a 6-inch silver wire segment, then twist them by twisting the wire ends together at the base.

3 To make the petals, take a 20-inch silver wire segment and make six rings of six dark pink beads each, leaving 4 inches bare at each end.

4 Now assemble the flower. Twist one end of the flower wire to that of the pistil, make a crown with the pistil in the center and twist all the base wires together to make the stem.

5 Make a branchlet by arranging flowers and leaves in small bouquets. Twist the stem wires together and cover with florist tape. Fasten each branchlet on a real peach tree branch using green wire. The illustration at right is one example of how you might finish this project: we set the tree in a small clay pot using plaster of Paris and covered the top of the pot with synthetic moss.

Red Rose

step by step

Time 5 HOURS AND 30 MINUTES

Difficulty

Materials

50G OF TRANSP. RED ROUND SEED BEADS

25G OF TRANSP. BI-COLOR GREEN 2-CUT BEADS

65 FT. OF 28-GAUGE RED COPPER WIRE

50 FT. OF 28-GAUGE GREEN COPPER WIRE

1 FLORIST WIRE

GREEN FLORIST TAPE

1 Fold a 28-inch segment of red wire in half and string three red beads to the center; go back with the wire ends through the holes of the last two beads and pull it taut, making a triangle.

2 At one end of the wire, thread four round beads and cross the other end by threading it through the holes of the four beads. Pull the wires until these beads are lined tightly below the two bottom beads of the triangle. Continue in the same fashion, increasing each round by two beads until you have a fan with an outer row of 18 beads.

3 Finish by threading 14 more beads on each strand of the wire, then cross the wires through the hole of the first, central bead and block by twisting the wires. Make five more petals following the same technique.

4 Prepare another set of six petals slightly larger than the first set. Each of these petals needs a 36-inch wire segment and will have an outer row of 24 beads, thus you will need to make more rows. The side row that closes each petal on each side as described in step 3, will also be longer so you will need more beads for it. Using the same technique, make a third set of six even larger petals using about 40 inches of wire each, with each petal having an outer row of 30 beads.

5 Fasten the petals to the florist wire, with the smallest ones in the center. After making the sepals as illustrated in step 6, complete the rose by fastening them around the base of the petals. Cover with florist tape.

6 Using 16 inches of green wire for each sepal, make six sepals with the same technique used for the petals, but increase each row by one bead until the outer row is seven beads; repeat four more rows of seven beads each; twist the ends together at the base.

Carnation

step by step

Difficulty

Materials

70G OF TRANSP. RED 3-CUT BEADS

50G OF SATIN GREEN ROUND SEED BEADS

30 FT. OF 28-GAUGE SILVER-COLORED COPPER WIRE

30 FT. OF 28-GAUGE GREEN COPPER WIRE

1 FLORIST WIRE

GREEN FLORIST TAPE

FLAT-NOSE PLIERS

1 Thread 14 red beads on the silver wire, leaving the first 6 inches bare. Twist the wire once and thread 13 more beads on each end. Twist the two ends of the wire at the base, thus forming this first petal into an elongated figure 8 as shown above.

2 Continue in this fashion along the same wire until you have a star with 10 petals. Cut the ends of the wire leaving the last 4 inches bare. Now prepare seven more stars.

3 Assemble the corolla by twisting the wire ends of each star to the florist wire, using the pliers if needed.

4 Now take the green wire and, following the same technique, make the first sepal of the calyx using 11 and 22 green beads for each figure 8 respectively.

5 Make 19 more calyx sepals. You can make them individually on separate wire segments or on the same wire. Finally, surround the corolla with the calyx sepals and twist the calyx wires to the stem.

6 Make the leaves using the same technique of the rose leaves (page 84). Fasten them to the stem and wrap it with tape. To keep the corolla tight, take 40 inches of green wire and fasten it to the twist between the two parts of the figure 8 of each sepal. Twist and fasten the wire on the same spot for the other sepals, making sure the flower is tight and secure.

Water Lily

step by step

Time 4 HOURS

Difficulty ● ● ●

Materials

8G OF TRANSP. YELLOW 2-CUT BEADS

12G OF TRANSP. ANTIQUE WHITE 2-CUT BEADS

40G OF TRANSP. FUCHSIA 2-CUT BEADS

20G OF TRANSP. LIGHT GREEN 2-CUT BEADS

50 FT. OF 28-GAUGE SILVER-COLORED COPPER WIRE

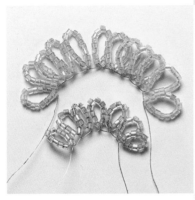

1 Take one end of the silver wire, leave the first 4 inches bare and thread the antique white beads on it, forming a crown composed of seven rings of 10 beads each. Twist the wire at the base of each ring, leave 4 inches of wire bare, and cut. Using this technique, make two more white crowns. Then make three crowns of yellow beads, each one consisting of 12 rings of 15 beads each.

2 Twist the wire ends of the three white crowns together to form the center of the flower. Then arrange the three yellow crowns around the white center twisting the base wires together.

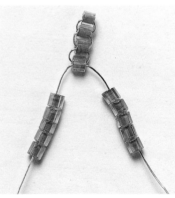

3 Take a 20-inch wire segment and bend it in a U shape at a distance of 8 inches from one end. Thread four fuchsia beads and cross the two ends of the wire through the hole of each bead, then thread five more beads on each strands of the wire.

4 Fasten each strand together with a twist, join them, and insert one bead. Now thread eight beads on the longer strand of wire, go back through the hole of the last bead in the first segment, and make a second arched row using eight beads. Thread one bead on the shorter strand and cross both wire ends through the bead.

5 Repeat step 4, but thread the wire back through the hole of the second bead of the initial segment. With this method, make two more couples of filaments, then thread the wire back though all the beads of the last filament. Finish by twisting both ends at the base of the petal. With this method, make 11 more petals – some larger by using six beads for the initial segment, adjusting the length of the subsequent filaments accordingly.

6 Prepare the leaves by making an initial segment crossing two beads at a time. Insert five more beads on each wire strand and continue as in step 4. Finally, assemble the flower.

Lavender

step by step

Time 2 HOURS

Difficulty

Materials

18G OF TRANSP. LAVENDER-BLUE 3-CUT BEADS

6G OF SATIN GREEN ROUND SEED BEADS

30 FT. OF 28-GAUGE COPPER WIRE

7 FT. OF 28-GAUGE GREEN COPPER WIRE

GREEN EMBROIDERY FLOSS, 1 FLORIST WIRE

CLEAR NAIL POLISH

2 Make another ring following the same technique: thread 10 blue beads on one end of the wire an inch or so from the first ring, and twist at the base to get close to the pinch on the figure 8.

1 Cut an 8-inch segment of copper wire and thread 10 blue beads, blocking them with a twist at the base. Flatten it, then pass one end of the wire to the opposite side of the twisted base, and pull to make a figure 8.

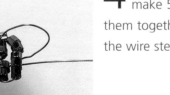

4 Using this technique, make 50 flowerets. Join them together by twisting the wire stems together.

3 Pass one end of the wire to the opposite side from the twisted base of the second ring and pull, making another figure 8; together with the first, you now have a floweret with four rings that you will shape by bending the apexes upwards.

5 Now make the thin leaves. Take an 8-inch segment of green wire and thread 21 green beads, then go back with the wire through the hole of the next to the last bead. This way, once you pull the wire the last bead will block the leaf. Continue to go back with the wire through the holes of the remaining beads and exit from the first bead threaded. Following this technique, make six more thin leaves.

6 Wrap the flower's stem and the leaves around the florist wire. Finish by covering the rod tightly with the embroidery floss and block the ends of the floss with a drop of clear nail polish.

Grape Vine

step by step

Time 7 HOURS

Difficulty

Materials

30G OF TRANSP. GREEN ROUND SEED BEADS

20G OF TRANSP. AMETHYST ROUND SEED BEADS

30 FT. OF 28-GAUGE SILVER-COLORED COPPER WIRE

50 FT. OF 28-GAUGE GREEN COPPER WIRE

7 FT. OF 9-GAUGE ALUMINUM WIRE

GREEN AND BROWN FLORIST TAPE

1 The vine leaf has three parts: we make the first by following the weaving technique we used for the red rose petals on page 100. Take 20 inches of green wire and make a triangle with five beads in the outer row, increasing each row by one bead only.

2 Continue weaving, this time reducing each row by one bead thus completing the first, rhomboid-shaped central part of the leaf.

3 Now make the second part of the leaf using another wire segment. Create a triangle with three beads on the bottom row and hook it to the rhombus, passing the wire through the loop of its central (five-bead) row. Thread four more beads and hook it to the next loop down.

4 Continue to make rows, decreasing each one by one bead and hooking them to the loops down the side of the rhombus. Make the third part of the leaf hooking it to the other side of the rhombus. To finish the leaf, gather the three wires and twist them together to make a stem that you will wrap with green florist tape.

5 To make the grape bunches, take 10 inches of silver wire, thread three amethyst beads, fold the wire in half, and twist the ends. Thread three more beads at one end and twist to join the two triangles, forming a tiny bunch. Twist the threads at the base to make a stem. Continue to make three bunches per strand, making them gradually larger by adding one bead at a time.

6 Assemble the parts: wrap the wires with green florist tape, and add small tendrils made by wrapping florist tape around the aluminum wire. If you don't have a real vine branch to use as a trunk, follow the procedure we used for the olive tree on page 96, and cover the aluminum wire with brown insulating tape.

Beaded Picture Frame

step
by
step

Time 1 HOUR AND 30 MINUTES

Difficulty

Materials

1 WOODEN FRAME

25G OF TRANSP. RED
3-CUT BEADS

RED ACRYLIC
PAINT

VINYL GLUE

BRUSH

SPATULA

2 In a small bowl, mix the glue with some paint. Spread small amounts of the compound on the frame and quickly apply the beads.

1 With this project, you will learn an efficient method for updating old frames that are in poor condition or no longer fashionable. Start by painting a wooden frame with red acrylic paint.

3 This done, use more of the paint-glue mix and more beads to fill any empty spaces or uneven areas.

Switch-Plate Cover

This is a cute project for a child's room. Use ¼-inch-thick pressed cardboard. Cut a piece in the shape of a house, also making a cutout in the center for the switch. Draw the roof, trees, and door; the cutout window in the center is for the switch. Work one area at a time, spreading colored glue and applying beads of the same color on top. Once done, glue the switch-plate cover to the switch-plate.

Lamp Shade

step by step

2 Spread uniform small amounts of the glue, one area at a time, on the shade, using a spatula.

Time 3 HOURS

Difficulty

Materials

10G OF TRANSP. GREEN 2-CUT BEADS

10G OF TRANSP. LIGHT GREEN 2-CUT BEADS

10G OF TRANSP. BI-COLOR GREEN 2-CUT BEADS

VINYL GLUE

SPATULA

VARIATION: LAMPWORK BEADS OF ASSORTED SIZES AND SHAPES

30 FT. OF 28-GAUGE DARK GRAY COPPER WIRE

65 FT. OF 1-IN.-WIDE SKY-BLUE ORGANZA RIBBON

1 Mix the three types of beads in a bowl, so that the colors will be applied uniformly. The combinations are endless, just try them out in advance to avoid unpleasant surprises.

3 Cover the glue area with beads, pressing with your fingers as necessary. Do one area at a time.

Variation

Here is a quick suggestion to update a lamp and turn it into an original piece. Wrap the lampshade frame with blue organza ribbon in a color similar to the beads. Secure

the ends of the ribbon with a few stitches. Now fasten one end of the matte-finish wire to the frame, thread one bead, and twist it to block it. Leave a few centimeters bare, thread another bead, twist, and continue in this fashion. Block the wire to the frame, pulling taut to form a net.

Flower Picture Frame

step by step

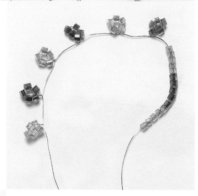

Time 4 HOURS

Difficulty

Materials

32 IN. OF 14-GAUGE ALUMINUM WIRE

25 FT. OF 28-GAUGE SILVER-COLORED COPPER WIRE, 25 FT. OF GOLD AND 40 IN. OF GREEN

15G OF TRANSP. TOPAZ ROUND SEED BEADS

10G OF TRANSP. BI-COLOR GREEN 2-CUT BEADS

8G OF FUCHSIA 8G OF PINK

8G OF TRANSP. BI-COLOR PURPLE 2-CUT BEADS

5G OF TRANSP. LIGHT TOPAZ 3-CUT BEADS

DARK GREEN FLORIST TAPE ROUND-NOSE PLIERS

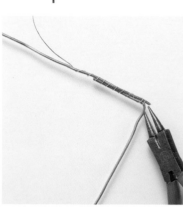

1 Using the aluminum wire, create an 8- by 6-inch frame, bending the corners to a right angle with the pliers. To close the rectangle, overlay the end part of the wire on the opposite end and block by twisting a piece of silver wire around them.

2 Make four small roses by using the gold wire. Follow steps 1 to 3 on page 84; then wrap the stem with florist tape. Of course you may change the color of the roses if you prefer.

3 Make three leaves using the green wire and following the steps for the rose leaves explained on page 100, then wrap the stems with florist tape.

4 Take a 10-foot segment of silver wire and make a wreath, alternating five-bead green and pink rings (remember to block each ring with a twist at the base).

5 Make the purple flowers following the procedure on page 122. Assemble the flower and wrap the stem with tape.

6 Attach all the floral elements to the aluminum frame, twisting the stems several times around it.

Purse Handles

step by step

Time 5 HOURS AND 30 MINUTES

Difficulty

Materials

25G OF TRANSP. DARK RED ROUND SEED BEADS

20 FT. OF RED STRING

20 IN. OF 14-GAUGE RED-COLORED ALUMINUM WIRE

FOR THE PURSE: 20 TRANSP. RED CRYSTALS

ROUND-NOSE PLIERS

NEEDLE

RED COTTON THREAD

42x17-IN. PIECE OF RED FABRIC, ELASTIC

1 Take the red string and thread 15 red beads. Make a cylinder following the technique for the tie knot explained on page 54.

2 Continue until you have a handle 10 inches long.

3 Make the purse using two 21- by 17-inch fabric rectangles. Decorate by sewing the red crystals on the front with cotton thread. Make a 1¼-inch hem, sew it, and pull the elastic through; block the elastic with a few stitches.

4 Take the red aluminum wire and with the pliers shape one end into a spiral.

5 Insert the bead cylinder on the opposite end of the wire and curve into a handle shape. Finally, shape the other end of the wire into a spiral as well.

6 Fasten the handle to the purse by stitching around the aluminum wire with small stitches.

Variation

For a simple, colorful version, make a soft multi-color cylinder handle without wire, using 20g of assorted-color round seed beads.

Beaded Scarf

step by step

Time 1 HOUR AND 30 MINUTES

Difficulty

Materials

6G OF TRANSP. AMETHYST ROUND SEED BEADS

NEEDLE

GOLD EMBROIDERY FLOSS

GRAPH PAPER

TRANSFER-INK MARKER

PENCIL

1 Before starting to embroider the design you have chosen, draw it on graph paper using a transfer-ink marker.

2 Transfer the design to the scarf, remembering to leave a ¾-inch border.

3 Using gold twist, embroider the design with the following stitch: come out with the needle to the front of the fabric, insert it a few threads back and bring it back up a few threads ahead; always insert the needle in the hole of the previous stitch.

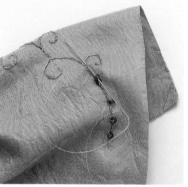

4 Apply the beads on the embroidered design, remembering to leave between the entry and exit holes a space equal to the length of the bead.

Hint

Beads are wonderful for rejuvenating old accessories. Make sure, however, that they are washable and choose only embroidery floss of the highest quality.

Alphabet Letters

step by step

Time 4 HOURS

Difficulty

Materials

5 FT. OF 14-GAUGE
ALUMINUM WIRE

30G OF TRANSP. FUCHSIA
2-CUT BEADS

30G OF TRANSP. PURPLE
2-CUT BEADS

30 FT. OF 28-GAUGE SILVER
COLORED COPPER WIRE

IRON WIRE,
ROUND-NOSE PLIERS

GREEN FLORIST TAPE

PENCIL
GRAPH PAPER

1 Make a 16- x 15-inch drawing on graph paper of the letter you have chosen. Following the drawing step by step, bend the aluminum wire into the letter shape. Block the overlapping points with iron wire.

2 Make the petals using 12 inches of silver wire for each. Thread 16 purple beads; twist the base to make an oval ring. Thread six more beads for a center filament; block it by hooking the wire to the opposite tip of the ring, then twist around the base.

3 To make the central button of a different color, make a four-bead ring, then a second ring with 16 beads, following the method for the wisteria leaves on page 90.

4 Assemble the petals and button to make the flowers; twist all the wires of each flower into one stem, which you will wrap with florist tape.

5 The final assembly: prepare a wreath with 25
feet of silver wire: thread five
beads and twist to make a
ring; thread five more beads
and continue to make rings at
regular intervals one from the
other, alternating the colors.
Fasten the flowers to the letter
at the proper points by twisting the stems around the aluminum wire. Finally, twist the
length of the wreath all around
the letter, thus blocking the
flowers stems more securely.

Flower Clothes Hooks

Time 10 HOURS

Difficulty

Materials

13 FT. OF 14-GAUGE ALUMINUM WIRE

20G OF TRANSP. PINK ROUND SEED BEADS

35G OF TRANSP. GREEN ROUND SEED BEADS

115 FT. OF 28-GAUGE SILVER-COLORED COPPER WIRE

ROUND-NOSE PLIERS

GREEN FLORIST TAPE

GRAPH PAPER

TRANSFER-INK MARKER, PENCIL

step
by
step

2 Make the three flower centers separately. Overlap the ends of each circle and block them with silver wire.

1 Make a drawing of the project on graph paper. Following the drawing step by step, bend the flexible aluminum wire into the contour of the design, using the pliers to make the curves. Remember to add 3 inches to the length of each stem.

3 Fasten each six-petal flower to its center by twisting silver wire around the contact points.

4 To make the wreath, take 80 feet of silver wire and thread 20g of pink and 20g of green beads, alternating the colors in five-bead rings. Leave the first 2½ inches of wire bare, then close the first ring by twisting it once; leave ½ inch free and make a second ring. Continue until you have used up all the beads.

6 Thread 12 more beads and twist them to the base; continue to make two more filaments, increasing the number of beads in accordance with the previous filament. Finish by threading the shorter strand of wire through the holes of the last filament.

5 To make the leaves, take 20 inches of silver wire, leave the first 4 inches bare, thread 10 beads, leave another 4 inches bare, and bend the wire into a loop by twisting it at the base. Now thread 12 beads on the longer strand and wrap it twice around the upper part of the filament.

7 Twist the leaf wires together into a stem and wrap it with florist tape. Make 26 small leaves following this procedure.

8 Wrap the leaves around the frame, except for the petals and the bottom part of the stems. Now cover the entire frame with the wreath. Using the pliers, bend the flower stems upward 3 inches from the end, creating the hooks.

Key Ring

step
by
step

Time 40 MINUTES

Difficulty

Materials

16 TRANSP. CRYSTALS

1 GALVANIZED
KEY RING

16 IN. OF
NYLON STRING

1 CRIMP BEAD

1 Cut 16 inches of nylon string, insert four crystals, then go back through the hole of the first crystal to the opposite side of the exit string, forming a small circle.

2 Insert one crystal on each strand and a third crystal through which you will cross the strands.

3 Repeat this step until you have 12 interlaced crystals.

4 Close into a ring by going back with the strands through the hole of the very first crystal, then go back through all the other crystals. Make a loop by threading four new crystals on the longer strand and block them with a crimp bead. Cut off the excess string. Finally, carefully insert the metal ring through the crystal loop.

Exotic Key Ring

To make an exotic key ring (which can also be adapted into an earring), join three feathers together with adhesive tape and insert a head pin through them. Thread the beads on the pin and curve the tip of the pin inserting the metal ring through it. For the earring, use an ear wire instead of the key ring.

Beaded Cord Belt

step by step

Time 3 HOURS

Difficulty

Materials

40 IN. OF THIN
HEMP STRING

60 FT. OF
COTTON CORD

1 GALVANIZED
KEY RING

30 TRANSP. TURQUOISE
GLASS BEADS (7MM)

8 ACID-TREATED TURQUOISE
GLASS BEADS (1CM)

ADHESIVE TAPE

1 Insert one end of the thin hemp string into the key ring to block it. Tightly wrap the whole length of the string around the ring and pass the other end of string trough the ring also. Then fasten the two string ends to the work table with adhesive tape.

2 Cut four 14-foot lengths of cord and fasten them to the ring with the same type of knot used for the macramé necklace on page 46. Bend the first cord on the left diagonally, laying it across on top of the others. Lift the end of the next cord and wrap it ring-like around the first (diagonal) cord, bringing it back flat on the surface. Repeat this step with the remaining cords.

3 Thread one bead on the second cord and one on the fourth, then fold the last cord on the right diagonally across the top of the others. Proceed as in step 2, but in the opposite direction: lift the end of the cord next to the first (diagonal) one, wrap it ring-like, this time twice around it and bring it back flat on the work surface.

4 Repeat the same step with the remaining cords. Continue to repeat step 3, alternating the direction. Each three passages insert more beads, always on alternating cords.

5 Finish by leaving a 20-inch fringe and decorate it with the acid-treated beads set at irregular intervals and blocked with a double knot on each side. Finish all the ends with double knots.

Write a Name

Time 7 HOURS

Difficulty

Materials

7 FT. OF 14-GAUGE ALUMINUM WIRE

30G OF TRANSP. GREEN IRIS ROUND SEED BEADS

35G OF TRANSP. BLUE ROUND SEED BEADS

50 FT. OF 28-GAUGE SILVER-COLORED COPPER WIRE

ROUND-NOSE PLIERS

GREEN FLORIST TAPE

GRAPH PAPER

PENCIL

step
by
step

2 Block the contact points with silver wire (for a uniform look, use some of the same wire you are going to use to decorate it).

5 Thread one of the ends through the bead-holes of the last ring and exit on the opposite side, creating one single horizontal wire.

1 Write the name on graph paper. Using the pliers, shape the aluminum wire to follow the contour of the name. Try as much as possible to get one single flowing line.

4 To make the center button, thread five blue beads and twist the wire at the base, forming a ring. Using the procedure to make the wisteria flowers shown on page 90, make two more, larger rings, blocking each ring with a twist of the wire around the base.

3 Using the silver wire, thread blue beads to make six rings of 18 beads each, twisting each ring at the base. Leave 4 inches bare at each end and twist into a stem.

6 Bend both wires on the back of the button and twist them together up to the center of the base.

8 Join the wires of button and petals into one stem and wrap it with green insulating tape.

7 To assemble the flowers, insert the button at the center of the petals, alternating the colors.

9 Wrap the stems of all the flowers around the contact points and cover them with green tape. Harmonize the arrangement by placing flowers on the curved parts also, alternating the colors.

10 Finish by wrapping the length of the name with a 20-foot wreath that you will have built by following the procedure explained on page 126.

Wreath

Time 6 HOURS

Difficulty

Materials

30G OF SATIN GREEN
ROUND SEED BEADS

20G OF TRANSP. BLUE
ROUND SEED BEADS

16 IN. OF 14-GAUGE
ALUMINUM WIRE

15 FT. OF 28-GAUGE SILVER-
COLORED COPPER WIRE

40 FT. OF 28-GAUGE GREEN-
COLORED COPPER WIRE

5 FT. OF IRON WIRE,
GREEN FLORIST TAPE

PENCIL

2 Block the two strands with a twist; join the strands together and thread two beads on it. Thread 10 beads on the longer strand, go back through the hole of the last bead of the first three-bead set and make a second row of 10 beads.

1 Take 28 inches of green wire and bend it in a U shape 8 inches from one end. Thread three green beads; cross the two strands through the hole of each bead, then thread five more beads per strand.

3 Block this row with a twist at the base; make more rows, going back through the holes of the subsequent beads of the initial three-bead set, until you have a leaf. Twist the two strands to make a peduncle. Make 15 more leaves.

4 To make the flowerets, take 20 inches of silver wire, leave the first 4 inches free at both ends and make eight rings of nine beads each, blocking each ring with a twist at the base. Twist the rings into a spiral and twist the strands together. Using the same procedure, make more flowerets, grouping them into sets of three and twisting the wires into a stem that you will wrap with insulating tape.

5 Wrap insulating tape around 8 inches of iron wire; wind it around a pencil to make tendrils, then gently remove the pencil.

6 Shape the aluminum wire into a circle, 8 inches in diameter. Overlay the ends and block them with iron wire. Arrange the floweret groups on the circle alternating with leaves and tendrils; fasten them to the circle with tape as you go along.

Doilies

Time 5 HOURS

Difficulty

Materials

20G OF TRANSP. ORANGE
ROUND SEED BEADS

20G OF TRANSP. GREEN
ROUND SEED BEADS

25 FT. OF POLYESTER
THREAD

NEEDLE

1 Thread five orange beads a few centimeters from one end of the polyester thread, then go back into the holes of all the beads, blocking them. Insert one more bead and pass the needle through the first base bead. Complete the round in similar fashion.

2 Now form five small arches: insert three green beads between the spaces of the previous round, then two orange, one green, and two more orange beads, hooking them to the second green bead of the previous arch. Complete the round, passing the needle back through the two orange beads and the green bead of the first arch.

3 Similar to the preceding round, make a new arch consisting of four green, one orange, and four more green beads, inserting the needle back through the green bead of the previous arch.

4 Complete each round, always passing the needle back through the beads of the first arch. For the next round, insert six orange, one green, and six more orange beads.

5 Continue to add rounds, increasing the number of beads and arches for each round. Following the illustration at right, try to reproduce the arch's soft contour. Place the doily on the table surface: it should lie flat, not curved.

Variation

For different shapes, sew small doilies together with beaded strings, as in the illustration below. Use this pattern to make a bracelet or other fashionable accessories.

Sources

Listed below are a few Web sites, magazines, and institutions that offer cultural background, useful information, and projects to stimulate your creativity.

General Beading Information

About.com Beadwork: www.beadwork.about.com

About.com Jewelrymaking:
    www.jewelrymaking.about.com

The Bead Bugle: www.nfobase.com/index.htm

Magazines

Bead&Button magazine: www.bead&button.com

BeadStyle magazine: www.beadstylemag.com

Lapidary Journal: www.lapidaryjournal.com

Inspiration

The Arizona Bead Museum:
    www.thebeadmuseum.com

The Bead Society and Museum of Greater
    Washington, DC: www.beadmuseumdc.org

NativeTech—Native American Technology and Art:
    www.nativetech.org/beadwork/index.php

Index

Accessories, 110–139
Alphabet letters, 122–123
Amber beads, 14

Bead caps, 19
Beads, 5
  advice in, 11
  background of, 12–13
  choosing, 14
  types of, 15–18
Bead tips, 19
Belts, 130–131
Bracelets, 24–25, 60–61, 64–65,
    68–71
Bugle beads, 14

Chokers, 26–27, 32–33, 62–63
Clasps, 19
Clips, 42–43
Clothes hooks, 124–127
Cones, 19
Cord ends, 19
Craft knife, 20
Crimp beads, 19
Crochet hook, 20
Crosses, 44–45
Crystals, 14

Doilies, 138–139

Earrings, 28–29, 56–57, 58–59
Ear wires and posts, 19

Florist tape, 20
Florist wires, 20
Floss, 20
Flowers, 81–109

Glue products, 20
Half-crystals, 14
Head pins, 19

Industrial glass beads, 14

Jewelry, 23–79
Jump rings, 19

Key rings, 128–129

Lamp shades, 114–115
Lampwork beads, 14
Lariats, 36–37
Lined glass beads, 14

Metal findings, 19
Metal wires, 20

Necklaces, 26–27, 32–33, 34–35,
    36–37, 38–39, 40–41, 46–47,
    56–57, 62–63
Needles, 20

Pendants, 44–45, 50–51, 72–73
Picture frames, 112–113, 116–117
Pin backs, 19
Pins, 50–51
Pliers, 20
Purse handles, 118–119

Ribbons, 20
Rings, 30–31, 48–49, 52–53, 66–67,
    74–75
Ring-size bar, 20

Scarves, 120–121
Seed beads, 14
Semi-precious stones, 14
Spacers, 19
String ties, 54–55
Supplies, 20–21

Tassels, 76–79
Thread, 20
3-cut beads, 14
Trees, 96–97, 98–99
Twine, 20
2-cut beads, 14

Wire, 20
Wreaths, 136–137
Writing names, 132–135